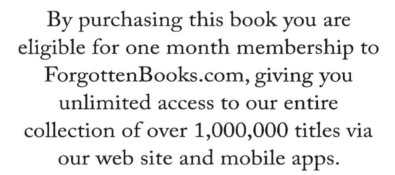

ISBN 978-0-265-58965-6
PIBN 10871791

Thesis

CHRISTOPHER MARLOWE: HIS LIFE AND WORKS

Submitted by

Margaret Irene Kenny

(A.B., Brown University, 1927)

In partial fulfillment of requirements for the

degree of Master of Education

First Reader Everett L Getchell, Professor of English

Second Reader: Arthur H Wilde, Dean, School of Education

OUTLINE

CHRISTOPHER MARLOWE: HIS LIFE AND WORKS

CHRISTOPHER MARLOWE

HIS LIFE AND WORKS

INTRODUCTION

"The life and death of Christopher Marlowe make one of the few dramas in our history which satisfy Aristotle's definition of tragedy. There is pity in the violent death that cut down such a tall genius in its youth, and terror for the faithful in the reasoned denial of God of which men whispered that the man was guilty. For three hundred years the tragedy of Marlowe has aroused a widespread interest. Curious fancy has spun unnumbered webs of theory round about the meagre accounts which have come down to us."[1]

But to understand these Elizabethans, and particularly Marlowe, one must come with a sympathetic bias and realize that these men lived dangerously. It is unfair to test them by modern standards of morality or restriant. "Men who were constantly face to face with violent revolutions of fortune, who were surrounded by a network of intrigue and espionage, whose words or actions might bring them at any moment to the Tower or Newgate, to the block or the stake, were not predestined to be patterns of scrupulous rectitude."[2] Not only underworld characters like Frizer, Poley, and Skeres, but statesmen and persons of quality like Thomas and Francis Walsingham, and Walter Raleigh, are far from conforming with present-day standards.

Even Philip Sidney in "Astrophel and Stella" sings of the charms of the wife of a rival. And Shakespeare - what of his dark lady of the sonnets? Does it seem likely that he "probably returned

1. Hotson, J.L. Death of Christopher Marlowe, pg.1
2. Boas, F.S. Marlowe and his Circle, pg.5

to his native town and home every summer or autumn for months at a time, and there prepared for the coming Christmas season, writing happily and swiftly in the midst of his family and friends?"[1] A Victorian among Elizabethans!

To come then to Christopher Marlowe, that "tall genius" that exemplified in his life and works the spirit of the Renaissance. Of all the great Elizabethans, he needs a sympathetic approach for he come "trailing the clouds of glory of the pioneer, of the herald of the full dramatic day. His is the magnetic appeal of genius cut down in its prime, with rich achievement, and with an ever greater promise unfulfilled."[2] Dying at twenty-nine, what might he not have achieved had he been granted Shakespeare's fifty years of life? That his genius was maturing, that the fiery temper of youth was toning down, we have his "Edward II" and "Hero and Leander" as proof.

But moderns love Marlowe for his uncompromising boldness in challenging the strongly-intrenched religious and political beliefs of his day. That his admirers are ardent and quick to defense, we know from the impassioned protests against the opinion of any man or document that tend to smirch his name. Thus the writings of Kyd, Greene, Baines, Beard and Vaughan have all been challenged for their truthfulness, and their biased unfair vindications, pointed out. When Professor Hotson unearthed the document containing the Coroner's account of how Ingram Frizer slew Christopher Marlowe "in defensione ac saluacione vite sue", many vigorous protests were urged against accepting it. Miss Ellis-Fermor in her "Christopher Marlowe"(1927) says that the evidence may have satisfied the jury but not Marlowe's present-day biographers, among whom there is the

1. Hotson, J.L. Death of Christopher Marlowe, pg.3
2. Boas, F.S. Marlowe and his Circle, pg.134

impression that Marlowe was murdered.

But he was truly a product of his times and he seems consistently to be presented as "a figure of passionate impulse and restless intellect, quick at word and blow, equally ready with the dagger-point and the no-less piercing edge of a ruthless dialectic. The combination in Christopher Marlowe of such characteristics with the dramatic and lyrical genius that created "Tamburlaine" and "Dr. Faustus", "Edward II", and "Hero and Leander", is one of the marvels of the English Renaissance. In Florence or in Venice, he could have breathed congenial air. It was Fortune's crowning irony that this most Italianate of Elizabethan Englishmen should have been born and fostered under the shadow of the central sanctuary of the Ecclesia Anglicana."[1]

In talent, temperament and tragic end, he was, in a sense, the Edgar Allan Poe of Elizabethan England. A poet of far greater poetic and tragic power than any of his predecessors or contemporaries (except, of course, the young Shakespesre) in his scepticism and curiosity a child of the Renaissance, but lacking Bacon's scientific balance and cool intellect, with a profound imagination of tragic hue, he came into the theatre from Cambridge University like a moody young Titan, not knowing quite how to use his own strength, straining in vain at the bonds of primitive theatrical form which held him down - and yet, as it proved, straining with such force that Shakespeare, his successor, could break them and free the captive drama into life.

Marlowe's contribution to English drama was not structural form, nor effective and plausible plotting. It was not even characterization, though its major heroic figures who beat at the bars

1. Ibid, page, 137.

of life, were splendid individuals. Character drawing certainly advanced with Marlowe, because he made the dramatic struggle within the soul of man, not against external forces. His great contribution, however, was the application of high poetic sincerity and insight to the dialogue of his plays, so that the speech of his people revealed their thoughts and their emotions with subtlety, eloquence and moving power. He could make their speech evoke a mood, reveal the torture in their souls (as "Everyman" hinted) or charm the listener with the rightness, the beautiful aptness of the words. He made poetry not an adornment and interlude of drama, but an integral element of it; he made dialogue alive and humming with overtones, a weapon for the dissection of the complicated human heart.

II THE MARLOWE FAMILY

The name of Marlowe was known in and about London favorably, for about a century and a half before the birth of Christopher. Richard Marlowe, ironmonger, was successively Sheriff of London and Lord Mayor in the reign of Henry Bolingbroke.

In Canterbury, the family was well established. Simon Morle, a vintner, admitted Freeman of the city 'by redemption' in 1438, appears as a leading citizen in the Chamberlain's accounts for the reign of Henry VI. In 1445-6 the corporation paid him four marks for a pipe of red wine given to the aged Cardinal Beaufort on the occasion of his visit to Canterbury at Christmas of the previous year. Two years later, he and John Shedwich were reimbursed 10L. which they had advanced as a present to the young Queen, Margaret of Anjou, at the time of her pilgrimage to St. Thomas the Martyr.[1] In the following reign of Edward IV, Thomas Marlow, roper, appears in the city records. He became Freeman by redemption in 1478, and in 1480 his name stands in the list of citizens occupying property belonging to the municipality, his rent being assessed at 6s.,8d.[2]

At this period, we hear of the couple who can be plausibly suggested as the great-great-grandparents of the poet: John Marley, or Marle, tanner, and his wife, Katherine.[3] In 1514, their son, Richard Marley, of Westgate St., succeeding to the title of tanner, was admitted Freeman of the city, 'by birth' i.e. as the son of a Freeman. Richard's will, dated 12, June, 1521, fills six pages and gives much information about his family conditions.

1. Hist. MSS. Comm. App. to 9th rep't.: 140,
2. Ibid, pg. 133.
3. Entered on roll as Freeman by redemption (J. M. Cowper, "Roll of the Freemen of the City of Canterbury", column 285, as Marle, John of Holy Cross Without, Canterbury, tanner, 1467.

The main purpose of the will was to provide for his sole living child, Christopher, a minor, When he became twenty-one, Christopher was to receive, besides the best feather bed and transon, 10 L in cash and other specified personal property, the whole of the lands and tenements subject only to a life interest in three messuages in Northlane, granted successively to testator's mother, Katherine, and the wife, Alice. Until Christopher's majority was reached, the major part of the estate was to be enjoyed by the widow unless she remarried, in which case the testator's representatives were to administer it for Christopher's benefit. The landed property mentioned included besides the three messuages in Northlane and Ruchard Marley's tanhouse, his principal tenement that I now dwell in' and 20 acres of land 'lying in the parish of St. Stephen's in the country of Kent, the which beareth rent to Sir JohnFfyneux, Knight (Sir John Ffyneux, 1441? - 1527, Chief Justice of the King's Bench)"[1]

Christopher Marley, son of Richard Marley, later married Joan Hobbes. Like his father, he did not live long and on 5 March, 1540, he made his will and last testament, describing himself as 'Christopher Marley, tanner, of the parish of Westgate, dwelling within the walls of the city of Canterbury,' and desiring to be buried, 'in the churchyard aforesaid (Westgate Holy Cross) next unto my father.' At his death, he left, besides his wife, a daughter, Elizabeth, and an unborn child, to whom, 'if it be a man child he leaves his dwelling place, and the hanging og the house, the meat table, the best chair, and a house joining my dwelling house called the Old Hall, with the land longeth thereto.'[2] No mean provision by the

1.Tucker-Brooke, C.F: Life of Christopher Marlowe, page 5.

2. Ibid, page 6.

standards of the time, but the widow received outright the twenty acres of land 'lying in the parish of Hackington, with the house and the meadow together in the said parish', and also apparently the tan-house which had supported the family for three generations. The unborn child, provided for in the will, may have been the John, who in 1564, became father of our Christopher Marlowe.

John Marlowe, Marley, or Marlin - for his name, like that of his son, is spelled in all three ways - appears on the roll of Freemen of the city of Canterbury as a Freeman by apprenticeship in 1564. "Marlyn, John, shoemaker, was admitted and sworn to the liberties of the city, for the which he paid but 4s. 1d. because he was enrolled within this city according to the customs of the same. 1564."[1] He was already married and the father of two children. The register of the church of St. George, the Martyr, contains the record: "Anno Dni 1561 .... The 22nd day of May were married John Marlow and Catherine Arthur."[2] Children of this marriage were baptized at St. George's, according to the church register and the archdeacon's transcripts preserved in the cathedral:

May 21, 1562 Mary, the daughter of John Marlowe.

Feb. 26, 1564 Christofer, the son of John Marlow.[3]

Dec. 11, 1565 Margarit, the daughter of John Marloe (Register only)

Dec. 18, 1566 Marget, daughter of John Marlo (Transcript only)[4]

1. Cowper, Roll of Freemen, column 212.
2. Catherine Arthur was probably the daughter of the Rev. Chris. Arthur rector of St. Peter's, Canterbury, 1550-1552. (Cowper, Our Parish Books, ii, 112).
3. "The 26th day of ffebruary was Christened Christofer, the sonne of John Marlow."
4. These evidently refer to the same child, one of the dates being erroneous.

standards of the time, but the widow received tri t the t en acres of land 'lying in the parish of Hackington, with he house and the meadow together in the said parish', and also apparently the en-house which had supported the family or three genera ions. The unborn child, provided for in the will, may have been he John, who in 1564 became father o our Christopher Marlowe.

John Marlowe, Marley, or Marlin - for his name, like that o his son, is spelled in all three ways - appears on the ro l o Freemen of the city of Canterbury as a Freeman by appren iceship in 1564. "Marlyn, John, shoemaker, was admit ed and sworn to the liber ies of the city, for the which he paid but 4s. 1d. because he was enrolled within this cit according to the custome of the same. 1564."[1] He was already married and the father of two children. The regis er o the chu of St. Geor e, the Martyr, contains the record: "Anno Dni 1561 .... E 22nd d y of May were married John Mar ow and Catherine Arthur."[2] Children of this marriage were baptized at S . George's, according to he church register and the archdeacon's transcripts preserved in the cathedral:

May 1, 1562 Mary, he daugh er of John Marlowe.

Feb. 6, 1 64 Chr stofer, the so o John Marlow.

Dec. 11, 1565 Margerit, the daug ter o John Marloe egister only)

D . 18 1566 a daugh er o ohn (Tran pt only)

Oct. 31, 1568	______ son of John Marlow.
August 20,1569	John, son of John Marlow.
July 26, 1570	Thomas, son of John Marle.
July 14, 1571	An, daughter of John Marle.
Oct. 18, 1573	Daretye, daughter of John Marlye.

Burial notices refer to an unnamed daughter of John Marlow (28 Aug. 1568)- probably Mary, the eldest child, of whom no mention is ever made again; an unnamed son (5 Nov. 1568) - doubtless the child who was christened only a week before and whose name was paradoxically forgotten by the recorder; and Thomas (7 Aug. 1570) who likewise died within a fortnight of his baptism. The baptismal entry in 1569 of "John, son of John Marlow" may be a clerical error for Jane or Joan (commonly spelled Johan), the daughter. There is nothing to indicate that the poet had a brother John, but his sister, Joan, whose baptism is not otherwise recorded, grew up and will be referred to later.

Shortly after the christening of Dorothy in 1573, when Christopher was about ten years old, the family moved from the eastern parish of St. George's to settle in the heart of Canterbury, in the parish of St. Andrew, where on 8 April, 1576, was baptized the last of John Marlowe's children: "Thomas Marley, the son of John."

The removal suggests increased business prosperity and is connected with a somewhat responsible avocation that John Marlowe took up at about the same time: that of acting as bondsman, for a consideration, in behalf of couples seeking marriage licenses. On 28 April, 1579, he first appears as surety on a marriage bond, being referred to as "John Marley of St. Andrew's, Cant., shoemaker". From this time until 11 August, 1604, he acted eighteen times as bondsman according to the extant licenses.[1] In these documents his surname is given fif-

1. J.M.Cowper, "Canterbury Marriage Licenses, 1568-1618."

teen times as Marlowe, Marlow, or Marloe, twice as Marley and once as Marlyn. Only in the first is his parish residence indicated; in the rest he is described, as if well known, "of Cant., shoemaker".

Christopher Marlowe's boyhood was spent in a house virtually without brothers,[1] but with four sisters, from two to ten years younger than he. They were still living in St. Andrew's parish when Christopher went to Cambridge, and in his second year at the university, his sister Joan, married John Moore, a Canterbury shoemaker, very likely one of her father's apprentices.[2]

Shortly after this, John Marlowe changed his residence again, to a house in the parish of St. Mary Bredman, and there took upon him the respectable office of parish clerk which he held until his death. The Register of St. Mary Bredman records the marriage of each of the poet's remaining sisters:

15 June, 1590, were married John Jordon and Margaret Marlowe.

10 June, 1593, were married John Crawford and Ann Marlowe.

30 June, 1594, were married Thomas Craddell and Dorothy Marl - .[3]

Note that Ann was married a few days after Marlowe's death; the family may not have known about it. In 1593, tragedy came in another form into the Marlowe family. Plague was rampant in Canterbury as in London, and at the close of the summer,it all but completely wiped out the household of John Marlowe's brother - in - law, Thomas Arthur (the poet's paternal uncle). The list of burials in St. Dunstan's Church tell the story:

Aug. 17 Thomas Arthur, householder

Aug. 29 Joan Arthur, a child

Sept. 6 Elizabeth Arthur, a child

1. It is not known how long Thomas lived, but he would have been less than five when the poet went to Cambridge.
2. Joan Moore, who seems to have married at 13 years of age, was probably the Joan Moore buried at St. Mary Magdalen, Canterbury, Aug. 19, 1598. She was dead when her mother made her will in 1606.
3. Last letters were undecipherable.

Sept; 13 Ursula Arthur, wife of Thomas

Sept. 14 Daniel Arthur, a child

One child, Dorothy, escaped and came to live with her aunt, Catherine Marlowe. She was mortally ill four years later, whereupon she made an oral will, giving all her possessions to her aunt Catherine.[1]

From this testament and from those of John and Catherine Marlowe, one gets on the whole an agreeable impression of the household in which Christopher Marlowe grew up. Nearly a dozen years after his son's death, John Marlowe dictated his brief will, signed with his mark, in which he asks to be buried in the churchyard of the parish of St. George within Canterbury, and leaves his temporal goods "wholly to my wife, Katherine, whom I make my sole executrix".[2] A few days later he died and was interred as he desired, the entry in the parish register of St. George's reading "John Marloe, clerk of St. Mary's was buried the 26th of January".[3]

Katherine Marlowe on 17 March, 1606, employed a scrivener of St. Dunstan's parish, Thomas Hudson, to write down her long will, disposing of much personal property, most of which is divided equitably among her three surviving daughters: Margaret Jordon, Ann Crawford, and Dorothy Cradwell. She also remembered John Moore, widower of Joan Marlowe and bequeathed silver spoons to each of her grandchildren. "Her son, Crawford" is made executor and residuary legatee. Like her husband, she signs with her mark. Though her request was to be buried in the churchyard of St. George's in Canterbury near "whereas my husband John Marlowe was buried", no record of her burial has yet been found.

There is very little record of the poet's childhood. But his being known as a cobbler's son gives no indication of the fairly

1. Brooke, C. F. T.: Life of Christopher Marlowe, page 12 – from "Archdeaconry Register, vol 50, fol. 361
2. Ibid, page 13 – quoting from "Archdeaconry Register", vol 52, fol. 373.
3. Ibid, page 13.

prosperous and important social position occupied by the family. "Marlowe, like Shakespeare, was born into the important leather-working branch of the old English guild system; but John Shakespeare was the citizen of a mean town in comparison with John Marlowe, who in point of fact seems to have been a prosperous burgher, maintaining respectable apprentices, marrying his daughters well, and ultimately leaving a comfortable amount of property and an admirable civic record."[1]

III. MARLOWE'S YOUTH

What meager references we have of the Marlowe family all tend to give the impression that their home life was of piety and tranquillity. Christopher himself was twenty-two years old before he renounced the career of clergyman for which he was destined. We can not tell the boy's dreams among the Kentish hills and fields, or beneath the jewelled windows of the great church in the city that not only still bore about it the lustre of its former sanctity, but was also the chief halting place of princes and ambassadors who journeyed from the continent to the court of Elizabeth. Perhaps these things touched him little; his own life was too vivid to be concerned much with antique sanctities. All his writings certainly reveal a peculiarly intense, full-blooded inner life, the quintessence of youthful desires and youthful dreams.

"It is easy to ascribe the Gothic gorgeousness of his fancy to the atmosphere of his natal city, with its rich architecture and hierarchical ecclesiasticism, its mediaeval pageantry and surviving Corpus Christi plays, its bull baitings and civic stateliness. But

1. Tucker-Brooke: Life of Christopher Marlowe, page 14-15.

Marlowe reacted against them really; familiarity with the ornate traditionalism of Canterbury ended by breeding in him a contempt, an iconoclastic intellectualism and modernist self-dependence. Probably he did not recognize these traits until well near the end of his stay at Cambridge and he had passed through the frothier manifestations before his death - but he appeared wilfully blind to the obvious beauties of Canterbury. Strange that he should speak of burning 'topless towers', of firing crazed buildings, and enforcing the 'papal towers to kiss the holy earth'."[1]

When he was near his fifteenth birthday, he was admitted to one of the fifty scholarships maintained by the King's school, Canterbury. We know nothing about his earlier education; he may have received it at one of those parochial schools kept by the parson.

In 1541, Henry VIII had given a charter of incorporation to a school in Canterbury Church - providing for '2 public teachers of the boys in grammar' and for '50 boys to be instructed on grammar'. The 27th cathedral statute provided that the boys be poor and 'endowed with minds apt for learning, who should be sustained out of the funds of our Church conformably with the limitations of our statutes: whom nevertheless we will not have to be admitted as students before they have learned to read and write and are moderately versed in the first rudiments of grammar, and this in the judgment of the Dean and Head Master ... And we will see that these boys be maintained at the expense of our Church until they have obtained a moderate acquaintance with the Latin grammar; and have learned to speak in Latin and write in Latin; for which object, they shall be allowed the space of four years, or (if to the Dean and Head Master it shall seem good ...) at most to five years and no more. Also we will that no one be elected

1. Tucker-Brooke, C.F. :Life of Christopher Marlowe, page 17

as poor scholar of our grammar school who hath not completed the ninth year of his age, or who hath exceeded the fifteenth year of his age."[1]

The accounts of the Treasurer of the Cathedral for the 21st year of Elizabeth's reign, 1578-79, are fortunately preserved in the Cathedral Library. These give for each of the four quarters of the school year the names of the fifty boys who received the quarterly allowance of one pound each and certify Marlowe's status as a King's (or, as it was then termed, Queen's) Scholar. The lists give in alphabetical order the names of Marlowe and his schoolfellows and show for what part of the year each held his scholarship:

Name		Rank in Treasurer's List, 1578-9			
		1st Term	2nd Term	3rd Term	4th Term
Emtley, John	______	4			
______					
Marley, Christopher	______		47	48	45

The number of scholars prescribed by the statute of Henry VIII was maintained and as vacancies occurred, they were immediately filled. Thus for the first time Marlowe's name appears in the second term, filling the gap caused by the withdrawal of John Emtley. Marlowe received his scholarship at the latest legal age and had actually passed his fifteenth birthday at the time he was paid two of the three stipends recorded. Unfortunately the Treasurer's accounts of payments for the next year, 1579-80, have not been found; there is no other mention of the poet until he is matriculated at Cambridge. Since he is listed at the University as holding a scholarship that was to be filled from the Canterbury school, we can assume that he remained in the school for the

1. Tucker-Brooke, Lif° of Christopher Marlowe, page 17

academic year, 1579-80. He probably went up to Cambridge at the age of seventeen.

IV. MARLOWE AT CAMBRIDGE.

Cambridge University Matriculation Book records Marlowe's matriculation, 17 March, 1581, as a member of Corpus Christi College: "Collegio Corporis Xristi. Chrof. Marlen". During his first term, (Lent, 1581), he ranked as a pensioner, entered as "convictus secundus", or second rank of students, intermediate between the fellow- commoners and the sizars. He was regularly elected to his scholarship: 'Marlin electus and admittus in locum domini Pashley'. His status was rather better than that of Spenser, Greene and Nashe, who belonged to the less favored class of sizars. A manuscript list of Cambridge students in Marlowe's first Michaelmas term - i.e., at the opening of his second academic year - records him under the name of Merling as a student of dialectic.[1] The students of each professor were grouped together by colleges, and the 'auditors' of'Professor Latinae Dialecticae Mr. Johnes' include thirty-one from Corpus Christi College, of whom the twenty-ninth is 'Merling'.

Professor Moore Smith's investigations have determined what the particular scholarship was that Marlowe held from 1581-1587. It was one of the three new ones founded by the will of Archbishop Parker, who died 17 May, 1575. The Bishop had previously given eleven scholarships in the college, of which five were to be filled from his native city, Norwich, or neighboring villages as stated, and two from King's School, Canterbury. In bequeathing money for the three new scholarships, he expressed the same local attachments. The first of the scholars was to

1. Landsdowne 33, document 43, fol.84 ff. (Manuscript in the British Museum, discovered by Professor Moore Smith.)

be elected from the Canterbury school and be a native of that city. Marlowe was the second scholar from Canterbury on this foundation. The nominal income of Marlowe's scholarship by Parker's will(3L. 6s. 8d.) was less by one-sixth than the allowance he received as a King's scholar at Canterbury, but he fared no worse than the average student.

"The Storehouse" fitted up in accordance with Parker's will as a chamber for the holders of the last three scholarships of his creation, is a ground-floor room at the north-west corner of what is now called the 'old court'. Here Marlowe lived during more than a fifth of his lifetime. The men who were awarded these scholarships were to be born of honest parents and were to be chosen between the ages of fourteen and twenty, being first well instructed in grammar, able to read, write and sing, and perhaps to write a Latin verse. They were to receive the stipend for six years if they should be disposed to enter into Holy Orders, otherwise no longer than three. No scholar was to be absent more than a month in the year and then only by leave of the authorities. The record of the quarterly payments given to the students roughly on a basis of a shilling a week for each week of the scholar's residence in college is a valuable record of the regularity of attendance of students. Marlowe can compare favorably with his companions in this respect. While an undergraduate, he spent an average of 47 or 48 weeks of each year in Cambridge. While allowed more freedom as a Master's student, he spent about 30 weeks a year at Cambridge during this period.

Marlowe secured his B.A. degree in the spring of 1584, at 20 years of age and after slightly more than three years of residence. In 1587, he applied for his M.A. degree. That he had studied for six years implied that he had intended taking Holy Orders, but for some

reason, he later changed his mind. Why, we can not even conjecture, but these forces determining his decision probably acted gradually and led to no flauntings of authority on his part. "Faustus' opening soliloquy seems autobiographical in its expression of the ardent scholar's slow disillusionment; and the total impression which the student of Marlowe receives is that he was the reverse of cynical in his attitude either to religious questions or to questions of personal morality."[1]

While it is probable that he left Cambridge after the granting of the 'grace' for the M.A. degree on 31 March, 1857, it would be necessary for him to return at the July Commencement in order to receive the degree he had earned. How he employed this interval has been an intensely interesting problem in research. Was it at this time that he wrote "Tamburlaine", which was a popular success by the beginning of the next year (1588), or was he a secret government agent?

There is a statement in the College Order Book that the scholarship had been granted to someone else, with no mention of the former holder, Marlowe. Dr. Moore Smith shrewdly thought this meant that Marlowe was not in good favor, a theory that was proven beyond doubt in 1925 when Professor Hotson found an entry in the Privy Council Register under the date of 29 June, 1587, concerning Christopher Morley. His contention that this letter referred to Christopher Morley or Marlowe of Corpus Christi College, and that he had been engaged on some government service during one of the periods of his absence from Cambridge after taking his B.A. - between February and June, 1587, - has since been verified by later research.

On the 29 June, 1587, the Queen's Privy Council wrote the following letter to the University of Cambridge: 'Whereas it was reported

1. Tucker-Brooke, Life of Christopher Marlowe, page 32.

that Christopher Morley was determined to have gone beyond the seas to Reames (Rheims) and there to remain, their Lordships thought good to certify that he had no such intent, but that in all his actions he had behaved himself orderly and discreetly, whereby he had done her Majesty good service and deserved to be rewarded for his faithful dealing. Their Lordships' request was that the rumour thereof should be allayed by all possible means, and that he should be furthered in the degree he was to take this next Commencement; because it was not her Majesty's pleasure that anyone employed as he had been in matters touching the benefit of his country should be defamed by those who are ignorant in th' affairs he went about.'[1]

In this letter we find him acquitted of any serious intention to go beyond the seas to Rheims, the hotbed of Catholic plots. Six years later we find Kyd accusing him of persuading with men of quality to go unto the King of Scots, 'where if he had lived, he told me when I saw him last, he meant to be.'[2] Evidently Marlowe's restless mind and reckless tongue got him into trouble frequently. But concerning this document, we may note: 1 - Whatever suspicion of Marlowe existed at Cambridge evidently came after his departure from the University , for on 31 March, he seems to be in good standing. Converts to Rome were at this time being made at Cambridge in alarming numbers; and as conditions then were, disclosure of the fact that Marlowe had definitely given up thoughts of entering the English clergy, coupled with a report that he was going abroad, would have been quite sufficient to start a rumour of his being converted to Catholicism. 2 - Marlowe's services must have been considerable in view of the fact that the Privy Council wrote the letter to put an end to the rumour concern-

1. Dasent, Acts of the Privy Council, vol.xv, page 141.
2. Thomas Kyd's Letter to Sir John Puckering.

ing him and the language used would lead one to think that the service was also quite worthwhile. 3 - He could not have been a spy or the government would not have been so anxious to spoil a rumour of disloyalty. 4 - It probably was of a moderately confidential nature, not secret enough to make it worthwhile to keep people in ignorance concerning it. He may have gone to France or Flanders on some secret errand; other poets are known to have traveled the continent in the service of influential nobles.

At this particular time, the political conditions were much upset because of the many plots to kill the Queen. It was not known whether France was actively involved or not; but it was certain that Philip II of Spain was preparing his Armada to attack England. There would be doubtless many opportunities to render service to the government.

Conyers Read in "Mr. Secretary Walsingham" notes that between March, 1587, and June, 1588, he(Walsingham) received from the Queen 3,300 pounds for secret service, a larger allowance apparently than he ever got before or after during the same length of time.[1] Perhaps Marlowe received part of this allowance for the work he did, but in that case he might have been recommended by Walsingham, a member of the Privy Council. However, Walsingham, the head of secret service and of English foreign relations, was not present that day the document concerning Marlowe was written and approved. Those who signed the letter were the Archbishop of Canterbury (Whitgift), the Lord Chancellor (Sir Christopher Hatton), the Lord Treasurer (Burghley), the Lord Chamberlain (Hunsdon), and the Controller of the Queen's Household (Sir James Crofts).

1/ Read, C. Mr. Secretary Walsingham, page 190.

Marlowe, it would seem, had an usually happy time at Cambridge for a poet. Aside from his failure to become a clergyman, as required by the conditions of his scholarship, there is no note of unhappiness or of insubordination. He kept his scholarship, gained his degrees and won an unusual recommendation of his character from the Queen's Privy Council.

V. MARLOWE IN LONDON

After taking his degree in July, 1587, Marlowe came to London, to throw his lot in with the dramatists, 'a boy in years, a man in genius, and a god in ambition'. We know little of the events of the less than five years and eleven months more of life allotted to him, except the very end. Most of his important works were written during this period. He is referred to as living in London or Kent, there being no record of visits to Canterbury or Cambridge. Neither do we know how he supported himself.

His output of work was not great compared to Elizabethan standards; Dekker and Heywood wrote as many plays in one year as Marlowe in six. Neither did he gain support by dedicating his works to the noble and the wealthy. There is no indication that he wrote catchpenny pamphlets and ballads, or that he wrote anything (unless possibly "The Massacre of Paris" and the York and Lancaster plays) with the careless rapidity of straitened circumstances. On the contrary, "the main body of his work, dramatic and otherwise, shows a finish and attention to detail unusual at the time; while the later productions, such as"Edward II" and "Hero and Leander", give evidence of matured thought and improved technique unlikely to have been achieved in so short a space of time without considerable opportunity for reflective leisure."[1]

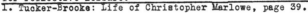

1. Tucker-Brooke: Life of Christopher Marlowe, page 39.

While Greene, Peele, Nashe, Dekker and Chettle struggled along in poverty, Marlowe seems to have lived independently and with well-to-do associates. His friendship with Sir Walter Raleigh and Sir Thomas Walsingham is well accounted for and seems to have been deeper than that of protégé with his patron. There is no evidence of his having been in their service or having received money from them, but he was on very friendly terms with them. Of his associates in London, Greene envied him; Nashe was his friend. He knew Chapman, Chapman's friend, Matthew Roydon, Thomas Hariot, the mathematician and explorer, William or Walter Warner, and the young publisher-gentleman, Edward Blount.

This was really the best company in England. Professor Tucker-Brooke says that to gain the entree into this group, some boldness was required, but that Marlowe had this in abundance. The clearest impression we have of Marlowe's personality is of an excessive physical and intellectual aggressiveness. He could talk with contemptuous irony, even when at Cambridge, concerning fools and folly; Nashe tells of Marlowe's referring to Gabriel Harvey's brother Dick as 'an ass, good for nothing, but to preach of the iron age'.[1] There seems to be no doubt that Marlowe had a fiery, impulsive temperament, but that it was also brilliant, we know from his friends and his own spontaneous flow of eloquence, and that he could brush aside obstacles in his striving for the 'unattainable lovely', we feel, from his assured grasp of his tools even in his first work, from the revolutionary concept his 'mighty line' brought sweeping in to the English drama, and lastly, from the unconscious identification of Marlowe himself with the great shepherd, Tamburlaine, strong enough

1. Nashe: "Have with You to Saffron Walden" edited by McKerrow, iii, page 85.

to master the Fates and bend the world to his will.

After going to London, he shocked the strait-laiced Kyd by his custom 'in table talk or otherwise to jest at the divine Scriptures, gibe at prayers, and strive in argument to frustrate and confute what hath been spoke or writ by prophets and such holy men';[1] and he ended by pouring out that combination of iconoclasm and fool-baiting nonsense which Richard Baines employed to prove Marlowe's atheism - affirming among other things, that the canonical estimate of 6,000 years for the age of the world could not be true, 'that Moses was but a juggler, and that one Heriots (Hariot) being Sir Walter Raleigh's man can do more than he', that all Protestants were hypocritical asses, and that he had as good a right to coin money as the Queen of England: 'willing them not to be afeared of bugbears and hobgoblins'.[2]

These statements come from men who wished to emphasize Marlowe's blackness of character and the whiteness of their own, but they nevertheless appear to ring true, although evidently composed of utterances of a questioning, restless spirit and casual deviltries invented for momentry effect. Kyd thought Marlowe reckless with his hands as well as with his tongue - 'He was intemperate (lacking in self-control) and of a cruel hart' and during the period when they were associated and'writing in one chamber', Kyd seems to have suffered a great deal both from horror at the dangerous things Marlowe would say and from fear for his skin when he reflected on Marlowe's 'other rashness in attempting sudden privy injuries to men'.[3] It was rather a case of Mercutio and Dogberry writing in the same room. Kyd was doubtless goaded, shocked, bullied and terrified: his sincere relief can hardly be doubted when, as he says, as well as by command of his squeamish lord "as in hatred of his (Marlowe's) life and thoughts I left and

1. Thomas Kyd's Unsigned Note to Sir John Puckering.
2. Richard Baines: A Note containing the opinion of on Christopher Marly Concerning his damnable ~~(opini)~~ Judgement of Religion and scorn of God's Word.
3. Thomas Kyd's Letter to Sir John Puckering.

did refrain his company'.[1]

Marlowe no doubt showed more genial sides of his nature to other associates than Kyd and the informer, Baines, But certainly since his departure from Cambridge and the public declaration of his good character, he seemed to have developed qualities of wilfulness and iconoclasm. It is an interesting fact that the first biographical document relating to him after the Privy Council's letter of 29 June, 1587, is a bond of 1 October, 1589, pledging his appearance at the next Newgate session to answer charges brought against him. Richard Kytchine of Clifford's Inn, gentleman, and Humphrey Rowland, 'horner', appeared as sureties for Christopher Marley 'of London, gentleman', each surety being bound in the sum of twenty pounds and Marlowe himself in the sum of forty pounds for his next appearance 'ad proximam sessionem de Newgate'. The charge does not appear. It may be that he had been accused of a breach of the peace and had to furnish security for future good behavior. No indictment or further action against him at this time has been found. There is no reason for thinking that the charges were related to his works or his literary career.

By the end of 1589, he was the author of some very successful tragedies, but he probably didn't reap much personal triumph from them. "No Elizabethan, in any word that has so far been discovered, has connected Marlowe with "Tamburlaine", though the author must have been fairly well known both to those who praised and those who blamed the work when Greene drew together his allusions to 'daring God out of heaven with that atheist Tamburlaine' and 'such mad and scoffing poets, that have propheticall spirits as bred of Merlin's race, if there be any in England that set the end of scholarism in an English blank verse'. "[2]

---

1. Thomas Kyd's Letter to Sir John Puckering.
2. Tucker-Brooke: Life of Christopher Marlowe, page 52.

In Kyd's letter to Sir John Puckering of the Queen's Privy Council, he alludes to 'our writing in one chamber two years since'. He says,"My first acquaintance with this Marlowe rose upon his bearing name to serve my Lord, although his Lordship never knew his service but in writing for his players; for never could my Lord endure his name or sight when he had heard of his conditions, nor would indeed the form of divine prayers used duly in his Lordship's house have quadred (squared) with such reprobates."

Kyd wrote this letter to the Lord Keeper soon after Marlowe's death in 1593 to obtain credentials of character that would reinstate him (Kyd) in his Lord's household. If we knew the identity of this Lord we would know for whom Marlowe was writing plays two years before his death. While the title-page of "Edward II" states that the Earl of Pembroke's men acted it, Pembroke's company is not mentioned before 1592 and there is 'no reason to suppose that it had an earlier existence'. Kyd's letter evidently carries us back to a period before the appearance of Pembroke's men.

Lord Strange is suggested by Professor Tucker-Brooke as the one for whom Kyd and Marlowe were writing. "The situation, as it relates to Marlowe, may be explained if we remember that "Tamburlaine" (as the title-page of 1590 tells us) was produced by the company of the Lord Admiral, Howard of Effingham, which later revived the two parts of that play, as well as"Dr. Faustus", "The Massacre at Paris", and "The Jew of Malta", at Henslowe's Rose Theatre. The history of the Lord Admiral's company is very obscure between November, 1598, when performances by them were suppressed by the Lord Mayor, and 1594. In the interval they seemed to have functioned in an unstable combination with Lord Strange's men, playing sometimes

together and sometimes separately. Edward Alleyn, the great actor of Marlowe's plays, called himself consistently the Lord Admiral's man, but the company to which he was attached was at this period most commonly referred to as Strange's. In February, 1591, this company (referred to under both names) acted at court and in the following spring they were giving performances at the "Theatre".

This is the epoch to which we are carried back by Kyd's estimate of two years' lapse since he and Marlowe had worked together. The break between Marlowe and Kyd's Lord took place, probably about this time and involved as its chief consequence that Marlowe wrote no more plays for Alleyn to act. The fact that "Edward II" and "The True Tragedy" were produced by Pembroke's men and never performed by the Admiral's is most easily accounted for by what Kyd seems to imply, namely, that Strange had been shocked to find his company (in consequence of the merger with the Lord Admiral's men) serving as the vehicle for Marlowe's radicalism, and had forthwith commanded them to break off relations with the 'atheist' - issuing the same order to Kyd himself, through whom possibly his Lordship may in part have secured his impression of Marlowe's pervasive influence. 'For never', Kyd smugly remarks,'could my Lord endure his name or sight, when he had heard of his conditions (i.e. character).'[1]

But Marlowe was not always the iconoclast and in the parts he wrote for Alleyn it is only fair to discount the concession he made to 'the robustious periwig-pated fellow who tore his passion to tatters'.[2] He probably wrote to give Alleyn the opportunity of disclaiming at great lengths. In "Edward II", he is the chastened poet, who consciously subdues his nature to that he works in, and subordinates sheer beauty of language to histrionic effect. Yet the

1. Ibid.
2. Tucker-Brooke: Life of Christopher Marlowe, page 49.

result is so dignified and expressive that it is unwise to think of "Edward II" as weakened in vitality. In this play and in "Hero and Leander", a new note of sane tolerance has come. This can only be an evidence of a change in the personality of the poet.

Marlowe did not write long for Lord Pembroke's company. On 23, June, 1592, the Privy Council forbade all plays until the feast of St. Michael (Sept. 29), but by the middle of August, 1592, the plague was raging. Plays were prohibited and play-writing was unprofitable for the time being. Actors and playwrights left London for the provinces.

It is thought that Marlowe spent the last few months of his life in Kent at Scadbury, the home of Thomas Walsingham. Perhaps at this time, he wrote the fragment, "Hero and Leander" which his friend Edward Blount later dedicated to Walsingham in words that express how deep an affection the poet aroused in his friends:

'To the Right Worshipful Sir Thomas Walsingham,Knight.

Sir, we think not ourselves discharged of the duty we owe to our friend when we have brought the breathless body to the earth: for albeit the eye there taketh his ever-farewell of that beloved object, yet the impression of the man that hath been dear unto us, living an after life in our memory, there putteth us in mind of farther obsequies due unto the deceased. And namely of the performance of whatsoever we may judge shall make to his living credit, and to the effecting of his determinations prevented by the stroke of death. By these meditations (as by an intellectual will) I suppose myself to the unhappily deceased author of this poem, upon whom knowing that in his lifetime you bestowed many kind favors, entertaining the parts of reckoning and worth which you found in him with good countenance and liberal affection, I cannot but see so far into the will of him dead,

that whatsoever issue of his brain should chance to come abroad, that the first breath it should take might be the gentle air of your liking: for since his self had been accustomed thereunto it would prove more agreeable and thriving to his right children than any other foster countenance whatsoever. At this time, seeing that this unfinished tragedy happens under my hands to be imprinted: of a double duty, the one to myself, the other to the deceased, I present the same to your most favorable allowance, offering my utmost self now and ever to be ready at your worship's disposing.

Edward Blount

If one were to judge by this letter and the state of mind pervading "Hero and Leander", it would seem that the gracious and tolerant side of Marlowe's nature was foremost at this time. In contrast to Tamburlaine's boasting:

'I hold the Fates bound fast in iron chains,
And with my hand turn Fortune's wheel about,'

there is in "Hero and Leander" the doctrine of self-surrender as essential to moral completeness:

'It lies not in ourselves to love or hate
For will in us is overruled by fate.'

"Hero and Leander" has particular biographical significance. It forbids us to believe that Marlowe was fundamentally or finally intemperate, as Kyd called him, or of a cruel heart. Nor can we easily suppose that its lyrical beauty was achieved while the author was employing his less poetical hours as a libertine or a revolutionist.

Aside from the heavy mortality of the plague, there was such widespread hysteria resulting concerning anything strange or unfamiliar that the Privy Council became over-zealous to weed out aliens

and atheists. The Council ruthlessly ordered killed men who held opinions that in the least manner caused suspicion to fall on the loyalty of the subject.

When Thomas Kyd was arrested on 12 May, 1593, in the height of this frenzy, for 'vile heretical conceipts denyinge the deity of Jhesus Christ our Savior', we can understand somewhat why this timid man was only too anxious to prove that these heretical documents found among his papers were not his at all, but Christopher Marlowe's. Kyd claimed, in his letter to Sir John Puckering, that the papers were found among the 'waste and idle papers which I cared not for and which unasked I did deliver up', having been unknowingly shuffled with his papers on an occasion of his writing in the same room as Marlowe two years pre-iously (1591). It is interesting that the writing of these 'hereticall conceipts' resembles very closely the handwriting of Kyd, who was a trained scrivener. He likely had more connection with them than he cared to admit at this time,

But they were not composed by Marlowe either, although no doubt they expressed his doubts concerning the divinty of Christ. The book from which the fragments are derived is a dialogue by John Proctor, "The Fal of the Late Arrian", 1549. "Passages like the last soliloquy of Dr. Faustus and the miraculous response to the invocation of Orcanes in 2"Tamburlaine" (lines 2893 ff.) are not consistent with the idea that Marlowe was a cynical sceptic concerning the doctrine of the Trinity; but there is abundant indication that he was stung by obstinate questionings from the time he left Cambridge without Holy Orders."[1]

The Lord Mayor of London had given to special commissioners the power to examine suspected persons, and had invested them with

1. Tucker-Brooke: Life of Christopher Marlowe, page 57.

tyrannical powers. On May 12, 1593, Kyd was imprisoned for being a revolutionary propagandist and the anti-trinitarian dostrines, being found in his possessions were presented as evidence of his evil religous principles and thus of his dangerous social influence. Kyd thereupon testified to Marlowe's responsibility for the heretical documents.

Thus on May 18, 1593, the Privy Council set about obtaining Marlowe's testimony. A minute of that date reads:

'A warrant to Henry Maunder, one of the messengers of her Majesty's Chamber, to repair to the house of Mr. Thomas Walsingham, in Kent, or to any other place where he shall understand Christofer Marlow to be remaining, and by virtue thereof to apprehend and bring him to the Court in his company. And in case of need to require aid.'[1]

Apparantly Marlowe came without giving Maunder trouble for two days later this notice appears:

'20 May. This day Christofer Marley of London, gentleman, being sent for by warrant from their Lordships, hath entered his appearance accordingly for his indemnity therein; and is commanded to give his daily attendance on their Lordships, until he shall be licensed to the contrary.'[2]

No doubt the warrant for Marlowe's appearance was the result of Kyd's information against him, and the Council's intention of questioning him concerning his alleged heretical views as a means to further revelations about the seditious disturbances for which Kyd was in jail. Marlowe himself evidently was not jailed, but was, on his arrival in London, given the courtesies usual in the case of gentlemen brought before the Privy Council to give information.

1. Dasent: "Acts of the Privy Council", vol. 24, page 244.
2. Dasent: "Acts of the Privy Council", vol. 24, page 244.

Probably Marlowe was not in a serious plight, even though detained, for unless his loyalty to the Queen were in question, he would simply be reprimanded for his heretical statements and released.

"For all his unseemly witticisms against the current faith, his remarks about the moral aspects of counterfeiting, and his conversational advocacy of the King of Scotland, Marlowe was not politically minded. He was by nature as much the reverse of the demagogue or inciter to mass-riot as of the religious innovator, and was one of the last men in London whom even his enemies could have suspected of pasting pro-British posters on the Dutch Churchyard wall. We have no reason to doubt that the Council knew this. Its two most influential members, Archbishop Whitgift and Lord Burghley had signed the letter concerning Marlowe that was sent to Cambridge in 1587; and the fact of his guest-friendship with Thomas Walsingham must have weighed with them as testimonial. It was the kind of testimony that they took most seriously."[1]

However, Marlowe would unlikely be granted such a stamp of approval on his character and conduct as he received in 1587, for during these five years in London, he seems to have built up a reputation for unrestrained iconoclasm and flippancies in his talk. He was looked upon as one of the leaders in the 'blaze of atheism which Sir Walter Raleigh was accused of fostering'.[2] Chettle in the preface to his "Kind-Heart's Dream" (1592) is thought to have alluded to Marlowe when he spoke of the playmaker 'with (whom) I care not if I never be' (acquainted).

In the spring of 1594, a formal investigation of this group led by Raleigh was ordered and witnesses called, but no penal action was taken. And probably none had been contemplated against Marlowe

1. Tucker-Brooke: Life of Christopher Marlowe, page 61.
2. Boas, F.S: Marlowe and his Circle, page 15.

in 1593. But Richard Baines' charges against Marlowe were serious enough: the document is entitled 'A note containing the opinion of one Christopher Marley concerning his damnable judgment of religion and scorn of God's word.' Baines accuses Marlowe of saying 'that the Indians and many Authors of antiquity haue assuredly writen of about 16 thousand yeares agone whereas Adam is proued (said) to haue lived within 6 thousand yeares.

'He affirmeth that Moyses was but a Jugler and that one Heriots being Sir Walter Raleighs man Can do more than he.

'That the first beginning of Religion was only to keep men in awe.

'That he (Christ) was the sonne of a Carpenter, and that if the Jewes among whome he was borne did crucify him theie best knew him and whence he Came.

'That all Protestants are Hypocriticall asses.

'That if he were put to write a new Religion, he would undertake both a more Excellent and Admirable methode and that all the neue testament is filthily written.

'That he had as good Right to Coine as the Queen of England, and that he was acquainted with one Poole a prisoner in Newgate who hath greate Skill in mixture of mettals and hauinge learned some thinges of him he ment through help of a Cunninge stamp maker to Coin ffrench Crownes, pistoletes and English shillinges.

'That on Ric Cholmley hath Confessed that he was persuaded by Marloe's Reasons to become an Atheist.

The last paragraph shows how deeply Baines was offended by Marlowe's rashness: 'These things with many other shall by good and honest witness be approved to be his opinions and common speeches,

and that this Marlow doth not only hold them himself, but almost into every company he cometh he persuades men to atheism, willing them not to be afeared of bugbears and hobgoblins, and utterly scorning both God and His ministers: as I, Richard Baines, will justify and approve both by mine oath and the testimony of many honest men. And almost all men with whom he hath conversed any time will testify the same; and, as I think, all men in Christianity ought to endeavor that the mouth of so dangerous a member may be stopped. He saith likewise that he hath quoted a number of contrarities out of the Scripture which he hath given to some great men who in convenient time shall be named. When these things shall be called in question, the witness shall be produced.'

This paper is signed 'Richard Baines' and endorsed, in writing partially illegible,

B (a) y(n)s Marli( )
of his blasphe
myes."[1]

A copy of this was made and prepared for Elizabeth and her councillors, but the heading was replaced later by another note: 'A note delivered on Whitsun Eve last of the most horrible blasphemies and damnable opinions uttered by Christofer Marley who within three days after came to a sudden and fearful end of his life'.

Commentators on Marlowe will probably never agree as to how reliable and trustworthy Baines' charges against Marlowe are. Certainly we know that Baines himself was an informer, a low criminal, who not many years after Marlowe's death, was hanged. And Kyd was a timid soul, "(a poltroon, I fear)"[2] anxious to redeem himself in the eyes of his patron; he did so at Marlowe's expense. We have all the

1. Tucker-Brooke: Life of Christopher Marlowe, page 63.
2. Boas, F.S.; Marlowe and His Circle, page 24.

weight of the opinion of President Eliot of Harvard on the side that Baines' declarations were hardly to be considered as true or just.[1] However, Professor Boas, in 1930, after much study and consideration came to the conclusion that all evidence points to Marlowe's fiery and impetuous nature, to his burning desire to break through restraint, to his restless, eagerly-searching, and scholarly mind; thus there undoubtedly was some truth back of these charges, even when allowances are made for the authors and their ulterior motives.[2]

VI. 30 MAY, 1593.

Marlowe, in answer to the Privy Council's summons, probably remained near London in order to be on hand when called by that body. Since the plague was still raging in London, it is not hard to imagine that he stayed at Deptford, about three miles outside of London. At any rate, there is no further mention of Marlowe's appearance before the Privy Council.

Because of Professor Leslie Hotson's discoveries, we know more of the last day of Marlowe's life than any other, though not enough to make everything clear. On the 30 May, 1593, he went to the tavern of Eleanor Bull, widow, in Deptford Strand, invited there to a feast, as Vaughan recorded in 1600, by 'one named Ingram'.[3] Professor Hotson discovered that this Ingram Frizer was a protégé or agent of Thomas Walsingham. It may have been that both Marlowe and Frizer were staying at Walsingham's home and proceeded from there to the tavern to meet Nicholas Skeres and Robert Poley. Although all three of Marlowe's companions were of some social standing and had influential supporters, they were hardly the best of company 'for a pure Elemental Wit', for they all had spent more or less of their time in and

1. Eliot, C.W.:Harvard Classics, introduction to "Dr. Faustus".
2. Boas, F.S: Marlowe and his Circle, page 25.
3. Vaughan, W: The Golden Grove, 1600, Book I, chap. 5.

out of jail because of fraud, cheating and spying. It is easy to conjecture, in the face of their past records, that not one of them would hesitate to tell a lie of any proportion to save his own skin. In fact, Poley went on record as maintaining: "I will swear and forswear myself rather than I will accuse myself to do me any harm."[1]

Frizer "was a clever and insinuating knave whom Walsingham assisted, with characteristic Elizabethan cynicism".[2] Skeres was a servant of the Earl of Essex, several times imprisoned as a seditious person. He and Frizer were at this time working together in several money-lending schemes for cheating foolish borrowers. In 1585, the name of Nicholas Skeeres was included in the list sent by the Recorder of London to Lord Burghley, of 'Masterless men and cutpurses, whose practice is to rob gentlemen's chambers and artificers' shops in and about London'.[3]

Robert Poley was the most interesting of the three - he was an adventurer and spy, working on a national scale. Even on this fateful day, he had in his pocket letters from The Hague to the Court, then at Nonesuch in Surrey. Professor Boas has discovered Poley's very colorful history and presents us with a man , apparently without semblance of conscience, utterly untrustworthy , but living by his wits and those of the sharpest, and yet, capable of enlisting the sympathy and support of the great leaders of the day who entrusted him with their most secret messages.

And these are the men, the sole eye-witnesses of the tragedy, whose testimony is to damn Marlowe as bringing the punishment upon himself by attacking Frizer first. As for the events of that day - which were unknown until Professor Hotson's discovery in 1925 of the

1. Boas, F.S.: Marlowe and His Circle, page 35.
2. Ibid
3. Brooke, C.F.T: Life of C. Marlowe, page 74.

El
ti
to
si
th
be
th

mu
Su
pe
su

of
in
to
cl
es
on
use
tof
hea
dee
the

Coroner's Report: Marlowe, Frizer, Skeres and Poley met together at about ten o'clock on the morning of May 30 in a room in the house of Eleanor Bull, widow, at Deptford Strand. There they whiled away the time (moram gesserunt) and lunched (prandebant), and after lunch were together quietly and strolled in the garden belonging to the house till six o'clock, when they returned from the garden into their room and there had supper (cenam) together. After supper Frizer and Marlowe began to quarrel, because they could not agree about the payment of the reckoning.

To quote Professor Hotson at this point:"Marlowe and Frizer must have known each other well, from their association at Scadbury. Such an intimacy helps to explain the quarrel over the reckoning. Companions quarrel much more fiercely than comparative strangers over such a thing."[1]

The coroner's report goes into detail concerning the position of the men and the events leading up to the tragedy: Marlowe was lying on a couch near the supper table; Frizer was sitting with his back to the couch and facing the table, while Skeres and Poley were sitting close to Frizer, one on each side, so that, he claimed, he could not escape when Marlowe attacked him from the rear. Probably all three were seated on a backless bench drawn close to the table, since few chairs were used in Elizabethan inns. Then in the midst of the quarrel, "Christoferus Morley" unsheathed Frizer's dagger and jabbing twice at his head, inflicted "trivial" wounds two inches long and a quarter-inch deep. Frizer, in panic, realizing that he could not get away from the poet's angry thrusts, grappled with Marlowe, got the dagger from him and 'in defence of his life, with the dagger aforesaid of the

1. Hotson, L: Death of Christopher Marlowe, page 54-5.

value of 12d. gave the said Christopher then and there a mortal wound over his right eye of the depth of two inches & of the width of one inch; of which mortal wound the aforesaid Christopher Morley then & there instantly died."[1]

Possibly more was concerned than the bill, especially since they had all four been in the inn from ten in the morning till six at night; and it was the custom for men to feast at an inn when discussing business affairs. Probably somewhat intoxicated, Marlowe and his companions were easily plunged in the midst of the fatal affray. One can easily imagine that such a virile and explosive temperament as Marlowe's would hardly let pass an attempt by Frizer to cheat him. Why Frizer's wounds were not of more importance is a point in question. Although he had been thrust twice in the head, so that the cuts were two inches long and one-quarter inchdeep, he could nevertheless turn about, held as he was at the table, and not only take the dagger away from Marlowe, but stab him over the right eye with such force as to kill him instantly.

Dr. Tannenbaum in "The Assassination of Christopher Marlowe" denies that the wound could have killed him and thinks that Marlowe was murdered at the instigation of Raleigh.[2] It is significant that the people testifying against Marlowe were anything but trustworthy characters, who might easily have made up this story against him in order to save Frizer's life.

However, both Dr. Boas and Professor Brooke are of the opinion that the coroner's account may be accepted as most likely the true one. They base their contention upon the fact that Marlowe did have a reputation for impulsiveness and rashness in a rash age, and that

1. Hotson, L: Death of Christopher Marlowe, page 33, quoting from the Coroner's report.
2. Tannenbaum: Assassination of Christopher Marlowe, 1928, page 38.

Kyd - after Marlowe's death*- wrote that Marlowe was intemperate and of a cruel heart, that he was capable of 'attempting sudden privy injuries to men'. Then, too, the officiating Coroner, William Danby, was Coroner of the Queen's Household and likely to investigate the presented facts thoroughly. There is no record of how the inquest was held or what witnesses were called. It is possible that others besides Poley, Frizer, and Skeres were called.

Marlowe was killed by Ingram Frizer on May 30, 1593. The inquest was held on Friday, June 1, and Marlowe was buried on the same day in the old church of St. Nicholas beside the royal docks at Deptford, and an entry was made in the Burial Register:

'Christopher Marlow slaine by ffrancis ffrezer; the I of June.'[1]

The jury returned the verdict of justifiable homicide. On 15 June, a chancery writ was issued to Danby, inquiring whether Frizer had killed in self-defence or 'feloninously and with malice aforethought'. On 28 June, the Queen issued her pardon to Frizer.

Four years later, Puritan writers took occasion to point out a moral from Marlowe's death, for they saw the obvious hand of God in this drastic punishment of the atheist. Thomas Beard, Francis Meres, and William Vaughan between 1597 and 1600 built up such myths about Marlowe, upon hearsay alone, that it has been difficult to break away from them. Beard maintained that not only in conversation did Marlowe blaspheme the Trinity, but even wrote a book against the Bible. No such book has ever been found.

"But see what a hooke the Lord put in the nostrils of this barking dogge: It so fell out that in London streets as he purposed to stab one whom hee ought a grudge unto with his dagger, the other party perceiving so avoided the stroke, that withall catching hold

1. Hotson, J.L: The Death of Christopher Marlowe, page 22.

of its wrist, he stabbed his owne dagger unto his owne head, in such sort, that notwithstanding all the meanes of surgeries that could be wrought, hee shortly after died thereof. The manner of his death being so terrible (for hee even cursed and blasphemed to his last gaspe and togither with his breath an oth flew out of his mouth) that it was not only a manifest signe of God's iudgement, but also an horrible and fearfull terror of all that beheld him."[1]

If Marlowe died instantly, Beard must have been wrong about the oaths and blasphemies, as Meres and Vaughan are equally wrong, or even more so, in their accounts. Meres in "Palladis Tamia", 1598, refers to Beard's account and then adds what must be an invention since no support for it has been found: 'As the poet Lycophron was shot to death by a certain riual of his: so Christopher Marlow was stabd to death by a bawdy seruing man, a riual of his in his leude loue.'

According to Vaughan, Ingram stabbed Marlowe into the eye in such sort that, his brains coming out at the dagger's point, he shortly after died. 'Thus did God, the true executioner of divine justice, worke the ende of impious Atheists'.[2]

But his grief-stricken friends are one in their note of sadness for his untimely end; here there is nothing but the highest praise for his ardent, generous nature and acknowledgement of his supremecy over them all in his divine gift of lyrical genius. To them, he was Kit Marlowe. Heywood wrote of him:

'Marlo, renowned for his rare art and wit,
Could ne'er attain beyond the name of Kit'[3]

1. Beard, T: The Thearte of God's Judgments; 1597, chap. 25 .
2. Vaughan, Wm: The Golden Grove; 1600, Book I, chap 3.

3. 'Hierarchie of the Blessed Angels', 1635.

George Peele, in a poem "The Honour of the Garter", dated 26 June, 1593, written to commemorate the investiture with that decoration of the Earl of Northumberland, bewails the death of 'liberal Sydney' and 'virtuous Walsingham' and continues:

'And after thee
Why hie they not, unhappy in thine end,
Marley, the Muses' darling, for thy verse,
Fit to write passions for the souls below,
If any wretched souls in passion speak.'

George Chapman, one of the continuators of Marlowe's "Hero and Leander", apologized for putting his signature to a subject 'On which more worthinesse of soul hath been shewed, and weight of divine wit,' and in his work expresses the hope that he may

'find the eternal clime
Of his free soul, whose living subject stood
Up to the chin in the Pierian flood,
And drunk to me half this Musaean story,
Inscribing it to deathless memory.'

Henry Petowe, also a continuator of "Hero and Leander", achieves fame only by his reverential lines towards the idol of poets' worship:

Marlo admired, whose honney-flowing vaine
No English writer can as yet attaine;
Whose name in Fame's immortall treasurie
Truth shall record to endless memorie;

Marlo, late mortall, now framed all divine
What soule more happy than that soule of thine?

What mortall soule with Marlo might contend,
That could 'gainst reason force him to stoope or bend?
Whose silver-charming toung moved such delight,
That men would shun their sleepe in still darke night
To meditate upon his goulden lynes,'

Even Ben Jonson said that Marlowe's 'mighty lines were examples fitter for admiration than for parallel'.

In "The New Metamorphosis" (ca 1600) the author, J.M. thinks of 'kind Kit Marlowe', who

'if death not prevent him,
Shall write her story: love such art hath lent him;'

Nashe, in speaking of Hero, recalls Musaeus, 'and a diviner Muse than him, Kit Marlowe'. Of the ardent admirers of 'kind Kit Marlowe', Michael Drayton in his Epistle to Henry Reynold's "Of Poets and Poetry" fitly describes his genius:

'Next Marlowe, bathed in the Thespian springs,
Had in him those brave translunary things
That the first poets had; his raptures were
All ayre and fire, which made his verses cleare;
For that fine madness still he did retaine,
Which rightly should possess a poet's braine'.

We would like to echo the sentiments of J.R. Lowell when he says: 'With him I grew acquainted during the most impressible and receptive period of my youth. He was the first man of genius I had ever really known, and he naturally bewitched me. What cared I that they said he was a deboshed fellow? nay, an atheist? To me, he was the voice of one

singing in the desert, of one who had found the water of life for which I was panting, and was at rest under the palms. How can he ever become to me as other poets are?'[1]

But no more appreciative and appropriate allusion to Marlowe was made than by the gentle Shakespeare who in "As You Like It" writes of his friend:

'Dead Shepherd, now I find thy saw of might,
"Who ever loved that loved not at first sight?" '

1. Lowell, J.R.: The Old English Dramatists, 1892, page 34.

VII. THE DRAMA BEFORE MARLOWE.

With the third period of Elizabeth's reign opens its most glorious period, political, and intellectual. One of the tendencies of the Renaissance epoch throughout Europe was the breaking down of the mediaeval hierarchy of classes and the substitution of a compact national body with the throne as head and centre of its life. While religious and political difficulties had created discord in England so that the nationalistic movement was partially checked, twenty years of Elizabeth's strong government had produced security and unity in Church and State. Elizabeth had the support of the great mass of the people; England was gradually but certainly emerging as a great power in Europe, of equal rank with France and Spain.

"The national spirit ran higher year by year, and found by itself splendid expression in deeds of adventure and daring. Between 1577 and 1580, Frobisher made his voyages to the northern seas; Humphrey Gilbert visited the shores of America; Drake sailed round about the earth. In the years immediately following, Raleigh sent forth his Virginian expeditions, Davis tracked his way nearer the Pole than any of his forerunners, Philip Sydney found a hero's grave at Zutphen. Then, to crown all, came the 'annus mirabilis' of 1588, when national life and death hung in the balance, and in the fashion as decisive as it was unforeseen, the scale dipped to the side of life. From the day that the Armada turned northwards to its doom, England thrilled with a patriotism as intense and operative as that of Athens after Salamis. And this feeling, ardent at all points, glowed, as it were, into flame about the person of the sovereign.

Elizabeth, to the men of her day, was no longer merely a woman or even a Queen: she became the incarnation of England, an ideal and romantic figure, a fount of inspiring energy. Such she remains to all time as the Gloriana of "The Faerie Queene".[1]

Such national enthusiasm arouses and stimulates a nation to a sense of power and strength hitherto undreamed of; the enthusiasm enkindled finds vent, partly in action and partly in artistic expression. Thus we find that in 1579, Spenser in his "Shepherd's Calendar" broke away from the restrictions of the classicists and compelled his audience to listen to the melody of English rhythms. Lyly and Sidney poured new life into the veins of the English novel. Stow and Holinshed, by the publication of their "Chronicles of Britain", gave proof of the renewed interest in the national annals; Warner in his "Albion's England" made these annals a theme of epical verse. Hakluyt, in putting forth his first collection of "Saman's Voyages" called the world to witness that all lands were full of the labors of his countrymen. It was inevitable that the drama should feel the force of the same quickening touch. History has shown that great dramas have arisen in different countries under different circumstances, but all have in common one condition - they have come in a time of intense national interest and effort.

Before the new learning of the Italian Renaissance had penetrated England, the drama had reached the point where secular plays (tragedies and comedies) were being produced with subjects chosen from history and legend. The people were used to scenic representations and had traced the outlines of what was afterwards to become the Romantic or Shakespearian drama. By 1576, permanent theatres were established,

1. Boas, F.S.:Shakespeare and His Predecessors, page 32-3.

a momentous event in the history of the drama for henceforth the patrons of the drama were to be not a select group, but the nation at large.

While at this point, Sidney, Lord Buckhurst, and Thomas Norton tried by their precepts and practice to introduce the classical style of dramatic composition into England, severely criticising the rhymed plays of the people, the involved tales roughly versified for declamation by actors in the yards of inns, and the incongruous blending of rude farce with pathetic or tragic incident, the people, with their eager, straining life, were careless of perfection. While the classicists delighted in tragedies like "Gorboduc" and "The Misfortunes of Arthur", which followed the model of Seneca and competed with famous Italian masterpieces, the people wanted vigor and movement, which they found in plays that were the product of untutored instinct, not of formal rule.

Thus a mighty impulse was given to the native species of dramatic art, and that in more ways than one. For authors, writing to meet a specific and immediate, rather than an occasional demand, threw themselves into their work with the energy usual in such cases. The very artlessness of the scenic arrangements gave to the playwright an unbounded scope. Time and place were at his command. He laid his plot in Scythia, or Africa, or Italy, without hesitation; his audience were ready at a word to follow him whithersoever he wished; they looked for no attempt at realistic illusion. Thus because the people rather than the learned were destined to control the theatre, drama advanced upon the romantic rather than the classical type of art.

What men like Sidney, Sackville, Norton and Hughes effected was in the main a heightening of the sense of dramatic dignity. They forced

playwrights to regard principles of composition, propriety of diction, and harmony of parts to some extent in the construction of both tragedies and comedies. Furthermore, they indicated blank verse as the proper metre of the stage.

The romantic drama - 'neither right comedies nor right tragedies', but 'representations of histories without any decorum' observed no rules and cared for no scholastic precedents. It only aimed at presenting a tale or history in scenes; and the most accurate definition of the plays which it produced is that they were stories told in dialogue by actors on the stage. Nothing that had the shape and interest of a story was amiss with the romantic playwrights and his manner did not greatly differ in the treatment of farce, pathetic episode, or chronicle of past events. This drama included chronicle plays on English history, biographical plays in the life of famous Englishmen, tragedies borrowed from Roman history and Italian novels, or based on dramatic domestic crimes of recent occurrence, comedies imitated from Latin and modern European literature, realistic farces, fanciful masques, and pastorals of the Arcadian type.

The one point which the dramatist kept steadily in mind was to interest his audience, which he did by exciting their curiosity with a succession of entertaining incidents. He did not mind mixing up tragedy with comedy, kings with peasants, and cared not at all forthe so-called unities of classical tradition. So long as he was able to make his audience feel the reality of life exceedingly and to evoke living men and women from the mass of fables which lay open to him from ancient, mediaeval and modern literature, he was satisfied.

These lines from Heywood aptly describe the vast tracts over which the dramatists roamed in their ardor for subjects:

"To give content to this most curious age,
The gods themselves we have brought down to the stage,
And figured them in planets; made even Hell
Deliver up the Furies, by no spell
(Saving the Muse's rapture); further, we
Have trafficked by their help; no history
We have left unrifled; our pens have been dipped
As well in opening each hid manuscript,
As tracts more vulgar, whether read or sung
In our domestic or more foreign tongue;
Of fairy elves, nymphs of the sea and land,
The lawns and graves, no number can be scanned
Which we have not given feet to, nay, 'tis known
That when our chronicles have barren grown
Of story, we have all invention stretched,
Dived low as to the centre, and then reached
Unto the primum mobile above,
(Nor scaped things intermediate) for your love;
These have been acted often, all have passed
Censure, of which some live, and some are cast."[1]

The material-groundwork for this great period of dramatic art came before Marlowe. Soon after 1580, the justly-famed "University-Wits" began to give high art to the romantic drama - such men as Richard Edwards, George Whetstone, John Lyly, Robert Greene, George Peele, Thomas Lodge and Thomas Nashe. Their importance consists in their contribution to Marlowe's style. "It was Marlowe who irrevocably decided the destines of the romantic drama; and the whole sub-

1. Heywood, T: An Apology for Actors (1612) Part III, page 35.

sequent evolution of that species, including Shakespeare's work, can be regarded as the expansion, rectification, and artistic ennoblement of the type fixed by Marlowe's epoch-making tragedies."[1]

VIII. THE DRAMAS OF MARLOWE - VERSE

It would be difficult to exaggerate the epoch-making importance of Marlowe's dramas. Without depreciating the efforts of the earlier Elizabethan playwrights, we can recognize the fact that they failed to point the way to a glorious dramatic future. The situation was beset with dangers and difficulties. The classicists frowned upon the romantic drama, yet the majority of the play-going public still enjoyed mere buffoonery and drollery, a fault for which even in later years they do not escape censure from the lips of Hamlet. Many worthy citizens objected entirely to plays, playwrights and anything else connected with theatres. Was it possible for a man of sufficient genius to arise victorious from the struggle against these discouraging influences and become the dramatic interpreter of Elizabeth's 'grand age'? By 1588, the question was determined, for in that year, Marlowe produced upon the stage Part I of his "Tamburlaine the Great", followed shortly afterwards by Part II. There is no hesitation in this first work.

In a few lines of prologue to his work , the young 'god of undaunted verse' announced his mission:

'From jigging veins of rhyming mother-wits
And such conceits as clownage keeps in pay,
We'll lead you to the stately tent of war
Where you shall hear the Scythian Tamburlaine

---

1. Symonds, J.A. (Introduction to Havelock Ellis' edition of Marlowe' plays,)page xiii.

Threatening the world with high astounding terms,
And scourging kingdoms with his conquering sword.'[1]

Thus Marlowe heralds his reform in the language and subject of dramatic art. With the 'jigging veins' of rhymsters are contrasted the Scythian's 'high-astounding terms', while his heroic exploits are similarly set off against the 'conceits of clownage'. Seldom has a literary rebel achieved so swift and enduring a triumph. Like other intuitions of genius, his new style was bold, yet simple. It consisted in the adaptation of blank verse, the accredited metre of the classical school, for the purposes of the popular drama, which had hitherto used the rhyming couplet.

"Such a change was absolutely essential if Romantic art was to attain to a rich and untrammeled development. Of all forms of literature, the drama, which calls its creations into independent life, and bids them be their own interpreters, naturally craves the largest and freest utterance. Its organ of expression must be stately enough for the highest uses, and yet sufficiently simple and nervous to render articulate the cry of the human heart in passionate extremes. Rhyming metres with their necessary element of artificiality and antithesis are unequal to the service; they throw emotion into leading strings, they distort its lineaments, dwarf its stature, emasculate its virility. Thus the genius of Marlowe seeking a fit channel of utterance, turned instinctively to blank verse."[2]

Twenty-five years before, "Gorboduc" had been written in blank verse and there had been other attempts to use this new medium of expression. On the whole, however, it had remained cold and artificial and ill-received. Its main appeal had been to scholars and

1. C. Marlowe: Tamburlaine the Great, Part I, Prologue.
2. Boas, F.S. Shakespeare and His Predecessors, page 41.

academic courtiers. To take this form and submit it on the boards of the public theatres to the rough and ready verdict of the pit, might well have seemed a hagardous experiment. Yet there is a tremendous leap from the tame pedestrian lines of "Gorboduc" to the organized verse, with its large, swelling music of "Tamburlaine".

The immediate success of "Tamburlaine" aroused envy in the breasts of Marlowe's fellow-dramatists. Nashe held up to ridicule 'the idiot artmasters who intrude themselves to our ears as alchemists of eloquence: who (mounted on the stage of arrogance) think to outbrave better pens with the swelling bombast of a bragging blank verse' and who can find no other vent for their choleric humors than 'the spacious volubility of a drumming decasyllabon'. Greene, running true to form, compared the metre of the play to the 'fo-burden of Bo-bell' and spoke with scorn of the writers who 'set an end of scollarisme in an English blank verse.' But Marlowe, sure of himself and his instrument, carried off the honors of the campaign so successfully that scorn turned to respect and finally to imitation.

This decisive result was due mainly to the transformation which Marlowe wrought in blank verse. The classicists had ended the line with a strongly accented syllable; each line stood by itself, separated by a pause from the preceding and following verses. The tame and monotonous effect resulting would have no appeal for the popular audience. Marlowe altered the structure of the metre, varied the pauses, and produced an entirely different rhythm of surpassing flexibility and power. Thus the 'alchemist of eloquence' transformed the leaden ore of the metre of "Gorboduc" into the liquid gold of his 'mighty line'.

It was not until later, however, that Marlowe realized the full

power and variety of which blank verse is capable. Although his early verses move with majestic power, their strong melody is simple and little varied; the chief variation is a kind of blank verse couplet, generally introduced near the end of a speech in which a tumultucus crescendo is followed by a grave and severely iambic line [1]

'And sooner shall the sun fall from his sphere
Than Tamburlaine be slaine or overcome.'

Extravagance of diction was common in the period and Marlowe was drawn towards it by temperament and by the special circumstances under which "Tamburlaine" was written. Rhyme being discarded, the poet sought to fix the attention of his hearers by strange, swelling phrases; it is not to be wondered at that this 'great and thundering speech' should at times descend into bombast and rant. Contemporary writers satirized the grandiloquence of "Tamburlaine"; Ben Jonson alleged that the language 'of the true artificer, though it differs from the vulgar somewhat, will not fly from all humanity with the Tamerlanes and Tamer Chams of the late age, which had nothing in them but the scenical strutting and furious vociferation to warrant them to the ignorant gapers'. Shakespeare himself burlesqued the speech of Tamburlaine through the mouth of Pistol, who directly quotes from Marlowe's play.

No higher praise could be given to Marlowe's contribution to dramatic poetry than that of Havelock Ellis: "In its later form, Marlowe's 'mighty Line' is the chief creation of English literary art; Shakespeare absorbed it, and gave it out again in his own great plays with many broad and lovely modifications. It has become the life-blood of our literature; Marlowe's place is at the

1. Boas, F.S: Shakespeare and His Predecessors, page 24.

heart of English poetry, and his pulses still thrill in our verse."[1]

Blank verse is essentially rhetorical, and consequently is indisputably the best of all metres as a means of dramatic expression. It can approach the prose of every-day life without losing its dignity as poetry; it can give the natural rhythm of conversation, and yet remain verse. When Marlowe flung to the winds all the rules previously binding blank verse, he made the emphasis fall naturally on the right words; the sound was an echo to the sense. The rhythm perpetually changed 'lift upward and divine', to convey the passions of Tamburlaine; swift, broken abrupt to ring the desolation, the despair that closes over Faustus, in that terrible 'last scene of all'; sonorous and sad to tell the tragedy of Marlowe's King.

Marlowe verse displays, especially in his best work, "Edward II" considerable variety. He handles the metre with consummate ease and the secret of his rhythmic effects lies in the skill with which the movement of the lines is always adapted to the subject. Here is a passage that is perfectly expressive of the easy motion of ships:

> 'Why then I hope my ships
> I sent for Egypt and the bordering isles
> Are gotten up by Nilus winding banks:
> Mine Argosy from Alexandria,
> Loaden with spice and silk, now under sail,
> Are smoothly gliding down by Candy shore
> To Malta, through our Mediterranean Sea.[2]

The labored effect of the third line is noticeable. The "Tragedy of Dido" contains at least half a dozen remarkable lines with the true Marlowesque swing:

1. Marlowe, C: Plays; ed. by Havelock Ellis, page xi.
2. Marlowe, C: Jew of Malta, I, i, 41.

'Then he unlocked the horse; and suddenly,
From out his entrails, Neptolemus,
Setting his spear upon the ground, leapt forth,
And after him a thousand Grecians more
In whose stern faces shined the quenchless fire
That after burnt the pride of Asia.'

I,ii, 1.183-8.

The resistless sweep of the verses, an effect altogether beyond the reach of Nashe, vividly reproduces the action described; even the epithet, 'quenchless' is characteristic.

It is in "Edward II" that Marlowe's power of writing vigorous blank verse in dialogue is best seen. His handling of the metre in "Tamburlaine" was a little stiff; the lines lacked flexibility. But no such reproach can be made about this play. He had acquired a perfect mastery over his instrument; the verse was supple and pliant in his hands. Throughout the play, the dialogue is quite strong, animated and firm.

Marlowe's creation of blank verse - for his blank verse resembles that of "Gorboduc" very little - was really a vindication of the dignity and resource of the English language and metres. He proved without a shred of doubt that there was no need of eternally appealing to the classics, that the revival of classic metres was futile, and finally that the English language was really a very effective instrument when handled by a man of genius.

IX. THE DRAMAS OF MARLOWE - CONTENT

Marlowe's plays may be easily grouped. "Edward II" stands by itself; it represents not only the highest development of the poet's genius, but what was practically a new creation of Marlowe's, the genuine historical play. "The Tragedy of Dido", left unfinished at his death, is rather a love poem, than a drama and may be classed with the poet's exquisite "Hero and Leander", both expressing in a high degree the purely sensuous Italian love of beauty for beauty's sake, which was typical of the Renaissance spirit. "The Massacre of Paris" is a mere fragment; the text is so imperfect and corrupt that for purposes of criticism, the play is wellnigh useless.

The three dramas, "Tamburlaine", Parts I and II, "The Jew of Malta" and "Doctor Faustus", are each a one-character drama. In "Tamburlaine" there is the great conqueror, who towers above all rivals; in the "Jew of Malta", we have Barabas, the protptype of Shylock; in "Doctor Faustus", the magician of mediaeval legend - each a personification of a single prevailing passion. Tamburlaine represents the lust of dominion; in Barabas, the thirst for gold is personified. Here is the outburst of grief when he realized he had lost all:

"My gold! My gold!. and all my wealth is gone!
You partial heavens, have I deserved this plague?
What! will you thus oppose me, luckless stars?
To make me desperate in my poverty?
And knowing me impatient in distress,
Think me so mad as I will hang myself,

That I may vanish o'er the earth in air
And leave no memory that e'er I was?
No, I will live. (I, ll.493-501)

So he schemes to recover his possessions and when Abigail throws him his moneybags, the intensity of his passionate joy is almost fiendish and uncanny:

O my girl!
My gold, my fortune, my felicity,
Strength to my soul, death to my enemy!
Welcome the first beginner of my bliss!
O Abigail! Abigail, that I had thee here too!
Then my desires were fully satisfied,
But I will practice thy enlargement hence:
O girl! O gold! O beauty! O my bliss!

Faustus typifies an incomparably nobler passion - the thirst for boundless knowledge. As Machiavel in "The Jew of Malta" says,

'I count religion but a childish toy
And hold there is no sin but ignorance,'

so too does Faustus. He is a very Paracelsus in ambition.

It is this all-dominating, overpowering passion that runs throughout all parts of the plays,giving coherence to all, and ensuring harmony of effect. It is in depicting the rise and progress of this central passion that the dramatist expends all the resources of his art. He shows us its beginning, a flame that slowly brightens and broadens until its fire, fanned by the wind, sweeps mightily onward, devastating all and at last consuming its originator. This pecularity of Marlowe's earlier plays is undoubtedly a source of weakness.

Marlowe is the most self-revealing of poets. The impress of his personality is stamped on every page with clear, firm lines; for the passions which his various characters personify seem to us at first to be distinct, yet if we look closer, we find in reality they are one and the same. They are different aspects of the all-absorbing passion that burns deep down in the heart of the poet, the flame that feeds on his soul. And that passion is desire of power. Tamburlaine craves kingship, because 'To be a king is half to be a god'. Again, Barabas loves his gold as he loves his daughter, but his passion is not petty or sordid, for he does not amass gold for gold's sake. It is for the power that money brings that he cares, and still more for the revenge it may give him on his enemies.

And if Tamburlaine and Barabas have their conception of power and, each in his own way, strive to compass their ideal, still more is this the case with Faustus. It is at power that Faustus grasps, and knowledge, he thinks, can give it, but not ordinary knowledge.

'Had I as many souls as there be stars,
I'd give them all for Mephistophilis.
By him I'll be great emperor of the world
And make a bridge through the moving air,
To pass the ocean with a band of men:
I'll join the hills that bind the Afric shore
And make that country continent to Spain,
And both contributory to my crown.
The emperor shall not live but by my leave,
Nor any potentate of Germany.

Love of the impossible - the search of the unattainable lovely - is the keynote of these three plays. It is likewise the keynote of

the poet's own character. One can trace in all he wrote the indefinable presence of one forever warring with convention. He struggles to be free. There is nothing petty in Marlowe's poetry. He soars aloft 'affecting thoughts co-equal with the clouds'. There is something of Shelley in him, for each was in a state of perpetual revolt against the tyranny of social custom and each might be addressed in Shelley's own lines to William Godwin:

'Mighty eagle, thou that soarest
O'er the misty mountain forest,
And amid the light of morning,
Like a cloud of glory liest,
And when night descends, defiest
The embattled tempest's warning.'

We see the revolutionary bent in Marlowe's character when he scornfully turned aside from the poetic form of previous dramatists and boldly struck out a new course.

What glory is there in the common good
That hangs for every peasant to achieve?

are lines spoken by the Duke of Guise and it is no less the thought of the poet. He blindly stretches his hands to heaven, and clutches at something 'that flies beyond his reach'. Marlowe was the incarnation of the spirit of the Renaissance, intoxicated with an unknown sensation of life, of power, yearning after he knew not what.

Thus Tamburlaine, Barabas, and Faustus are not the offspring of a purely creative imagination; they are rather projections from the poet's own soul. There is no gulf between the poet and the beings he paints in his poetry; rather, he is merged in them. When Marlowe goes outside of himself and has recourse to the purely imaginative faculty, he is not so successful. The other figures in his dramas

are mere shadows. Neither did he succeed in drawing a female character. Greene was the first to be able to depict women at all comparable to those of Shakespeare.'He rarely described the external world of men and women; he had little of Ben Jonson's precise observation and nothing of Shakespeare's gentle laughter.'[1] He showed a remarkable poverty in inventiveness, in the inexhaustible fancy of Greene. Rather, his effects were achieved by broad, sweeping dashes of paint upon the canvas.

1. C. Marlowe: Works, ed. by Havelock Ellis, page xxii.

X. THE TWO TRAGICALL DISCOURSES OF MIGHTY TAMBURLAINE, THE SCYTHIAN SHEPHERD. PARTS I AND II.

A. Date and Authorship of "Tamburlaine"

About the year 1587, "Tamburlaine, the Great" appeared, and the second part very shortly afterwards, in the spring or early summer of 1588. The play was very popular, and according to Thomas Heywood, the famous actor, Alleyn, in this play and in "The Jew of Malta", won the 'attribute of peerless'. It was entered in Stationers' Register in 1590, and again in 1592, the publisher in both cases being Richard Jones, who announces in his epistle that he had omitted 'some fond and frivolous Iestures'. We have no way of knowing how great the omissions were; certainly in their present form, the plays have little claim to the title of 'commicall discourses' (as first known), even when we allow for Elizabethan roughness of definition.

The first performance of which there is any record runs from August 28, 1594, onwards. However, from contemporary allusions that the play was known before 1590, and upon the most definite allusion, that of the preface to Greene's 'Perimedes, the Blacke-Smith' (1588) the arguments for dating the play have depended. Greene ridicules the popular tragedy of that time, 'daring God out of heauen with that Atheist Tamburlan' and goes on to say scathing things of the 'mad and scoffing poets, that haue propheticall spirits, as bred of Merlin's race, if there be anye in England that set the end of scollarisme in an English blanck verse ....'[1] The first allusion is pretty clearly to Tamburlaine's speech in Act 5 of the second part, while the words, 'Merlin's race' are a punning reference to 'Marlin', the common Elizabethan variation of Marlowe's name. It seems difficult

1. Greene, R: Perimedes the Black-Smith, (1588) Preface, page ix.

to escape from the conclusion that Greene referred here to Marlowe and his play.

There is no documentary evidence to establish their authenticity. The title-pages of the early editions bear no author's name and among the many allusions to these plays prior to the Restoration, there is no hint of their origin. But it is not surprising for an Elizabethan poet to fail to lay claim to his first experiment in a not very aristocratic species of literature, even after it had achieved success. Such critics as Dyce and Bullen accepted unhesitatingly the belief that Marlowe was the author, relying upon the evidence of its style and thought. For the personality of the author pervades throughout these plays. We are not merely assured that no poet except Marlowe was desirous or capable, about 1587, of starting the dramatic and stylistic revolution which "Tamburlaine" inaugurated; we see also that the individual artistic development which we can trace backwards from "Edward II" to "Doctor Faustus" must inevitably have had its rise in "Tamburlaine".

B. Source

The original Timur Khan (1336-1405) belonged by race to the group of western Tartars who fell apart from the main body when the great empire founded by Jenghis and brought to its height by Kublai disintegrated after his death. Timur seems to have possessed some of the qualities of both the great Khans of the earlier empire, the ferocity, tenacity, courage and military genius of Jenghis, the love of splendor and the capacity for government in time of peace which were a part of the noble character of Kublai. After a youth of struggles with rival leaders and Mongolian tribes in the neighborhood of

Samarquand, he had, by the year 1369, consolidated a kingdom for himself in the territory east of the Caspian sea. With this as a base he proceeded to the conquest of northern India and thence to that of Anatolia (roughly the modern Asia Minor) and Persia. In the year 1402, he met and overthrew Bajazet, the head of the Turkish empire, at Ancora in Bithynia and was proceeding against the southern Chinese Empire when he died in 1405. His character, as it was revealed by the Arab, Persian and Syrian historians, was a strange mixture of oriental profusian and subtlety with barbarianism.

The problem of the source of these plays is not entirely solved but Pedro Mexia's "Silva de varia lection" (1542) and Petrus Perondinus' "Magni Tamerlania Scythiarum Imperatoris Vita" (1553) undoubtedly are the written sources.[1] Probably Marlowe knew Mexia's work through the translation "Foreste" by Fortescue (1571). It would seem probable that Thomas Newton's "Notable History of the Saracens" (1575) furnished Marlowe with a number of proper names and suggested the story of Sigismund in Part II, while Herford and Wagner have shown that individual passages in Part I are taken in all probability from the Latin of Petrus Perondinus (1553). The second part of "Tamburlaine" is confessedly an aftermath, not contemplated when the first was written, and mostly Marlowe's invention. The story of Olympia was taken from Ariosto (Orlando Furiosa, Book XXIX).

Marlowe takes from his sources the salient elements of the career of Tamburlaine, simplifying and condensing so as to give the clear impression of a swift and unchecked rise surmounting by its power all opposition until opposition itself falters and Tamburlaine moves through a world of subject kings and prostrate empires. He omits all those episodes that lie outside this. Thus the early years

---

1. C. Marlowe: Works, ed. by C.F. [illegible] Brooke, page 9[illegible].

of Timur are only hinted at and the events that followed his death, the break-up of his empire are but dimly forecast in the characters of his three sons.

He passes directly from the winning of Theridamis to the preparations against Bajazet, omitting a list of minor conquests which would clog the action and take from the effect of Tamburlaine's comet-like movements. His is a magnificent but dizzy progress. All that could diminish or humanize him by partial failure is stripped away. The character of Tamburlaine is isolated in its fearless splendor, and its insolence and its command. No man, in the first part of the play, criticizes; all are sunk in a profound, mesmeric adoration.

Marlowe likewise alters the character of Bajazet, for in the poet's eyes, he is merely a foil for Tamburlaine. Whereas history paints him as valorous, proud and dignified, Marlowe presents him as a self-indulgent, headstrong Oriental, thus leaving Tamburlaine secure in our undivided sympathy.

"Such modifications as Marlowe makes tend to simplify the story and to make the figure of Tamburlaine stand out clearly from its background. This is the natural process of Marlowe's intellect, and it is precisely how we should expect to find him handling a large mass of somewhat amorphous material, reducing it to clarity, to shapeliness and to the service of one strong clear thought. When he is writing freely he does not reproduce his sources. He finds in certain records a figure, a series of events, a situation which seems shaped by nature to hold or almost to hold his own burning thought, The figure, the event, is informed with the thought, and behold, the place that knew it knows it no more; it is not Mexia or Perondinus but the idea of which they had been but faint reflections." [1.]

1. Ellis-Fermor, W.M. :"Tqmburlaine, the Great", page 59

C. Part II - Additional Sources

Of the events and episodes available to Marlowe when he wrote the first part of"Tamburlaine", very few had been omitted. There was consequently, little left of the original legend when a second part was to be written. He had, beyond doubt, a clear conception of the development the chief character should suffer, and this differed so far from the conception of the first part as to endanger the effectiveness of a play written on similar lines. His sympathies and comments seem to indicate that he was not so interested as he had formerly been. He seems driven to eke out his material by introducing irrelevant episodes, some of which he weaves in skilfully, others of which are, and look like, padding. The chief one of these is an elaborate sub-plot, the series of episodes whereby Orcanes, now the Turkish leader, enters into a peace treaty with Sigismund of Hungary and the European Christians, is betrayed and taken in the rear by them, yet nevertheless defeats them in the battle they had sacrificed their honor to bring about. It all seems a little irrelevant both to the action and to the general sentiment of the play, for Orcanes' triumph serves few purposes in the narrative; it does not serve to make him appear a great potentate and his subsequent defeat by Tamburlaine is expected before it comes, while his rather suggestive speeches on treachery and the chivalric law of arms make a jarring contrast with the frivolous mood of the scenes in which he and the other captive kings ultimately appear. This is partly because Marlowe follows his sources fairly closely for the details of the episodes without regarding the effect which the episode would have upon the continuity of sentiment or action. The source was the account of Bonfinus , "Antonii Bonfinii Rerum Ungaricarum decades quattuor"

(1543) supplanted by Callimachus, "Callimachi Experientis de clade Varnensi" (1556). This was reprinted in "Turcicorum Chronicorum Tonii Duo ..." of Philippus Lonicerus (1578).[1] These accounts, but particularly that of Bonfinus, are closely followed by Marlowe.

The escape of Callapine, who is defeated in the last Act but saves his life through the death of Tamburlaine, is generally referred to in many histories of Bajazet's life and is very slightly treated by Marlowe. It bears little connection with other episodes of the play, most of which are similarly borrowed and loosely affiliated to Tamburlaine without any further linking together. The figure of Calyphas is Marlowe's own; here is the hint of degeneracy that biographers had assigned to the sons of Tamburlaine.

One other source of "Tamburlaine" remains - and that is the source of Marlowe's geographical information. Since he had Zanzibar on the west coast of Africa and the Danube flowing into the Mediterranean, it was concluded by 19th century critics that his geographical knowledge was slight, and largely imaginary. It was not until Miss Ethel Seaton's researches on "Tamburlaine" led her to investigate more fully that the true state of affairs was discovered and Marlowe's fine scholarly mind fully appreciated. She found that when the place-names of "Tamburlaine", particularly of the second part, are checked against those of the Elizabethan cartographers whose works Marlowe might have consulted, it becomes clear that Ortelius, the compiler of "Theatrum Orbis Terrarum", is the immediate source of much of Marlowe's information, including the curious fact that Zanzibar is a West African district. In her study of "Marlowe's Map", Miss Seaton explained away these discrepancies, traced the cam-

1. E.Seaton, Times Lit. Supp., June 16, 1921, page 388.

paigns of Tamburlaine and of his adversaries, and in every case in which Marlowe's accuracy has been called in questioned, pointed to Ortelius as the source which he followed faithfully.

"As we follow these tracks through the "Threatrum", the conviction grows that Marlowe used this source at least with the accuracy of a scholar and the common sense of a merchant-venturer, as well as with the imagination of a poet. The assurance is that it supports the growing belief, expressed by such a critic as Swinburne, and by such an authority on Marlowe as Professor Tucker-Brooke that he was something more than a dramatist of swashbuckling violence and chaotic inconsequence - a 'Miles Gloriosus' of English drama. Here we find order for chaos, something of the delicate precision of the draughtsman, for the crude formlessness of the impressionist. Panoramic though his treatment may be, there is method in his seven-league-booted strides. We wrong Marlowe if, in our eagerness to praise his high moments of poetic inspiration, we mistakenly depreciate his qualities of intellect, of mental curiosity and logical construction. We do him wrong, being so majestical, to see in him only this show of violence."[1]

"Marlowe's absorption in what he read seems to have been as profound, his memories as clear-cut, as that of the most precise scholar among his contemporaries, whether the object of his study were a record, a poem, or a map. His numerous allusions in "Tamburlaine" to single phrases and details of Ovid's work would alone be enough to support this, were it not substantiated by the evidence of his treatment of the maps of Ortelius and his memory of the works of Virgil, Cicero, Lucan, Horace and of the special records upon which he drew for his other plays. But accuracy of study and reten-

1. E. Seaton: Marlowe's Map, page 34.

tiveness of memory is one thing, the free imaginative handling of what has been so retained, another and a rarer. In thinking of the process of Marlowe's mind, it must never be forgotten that he combines the scientific precision of a fine scholar with the wide imaginative scope of a great poet, a combination rare at all times, and among Elizabethans perhaps only possessed in greater degree by Milton."[1]

D. Criticism of "Tamburlaine"

In Timur, as later is Faustus, Marlowe finds a mind tuned as his own to the beauty and terror that besets man on that strange journey which is his destiny. Youth and power radiate from Marlowe only as they do in such a giant as Timur. Time and space are obliterated between these two strange spirits that 'look out upon the winds with glorious fear' and in this breathless joy, Marlowe creates the Tamburlaine of the play.

Tamburlaine embodies at first the poet's conception of the life of action, exhilaration and conquest that brushes aside obstacles hampering the ordinary man; the crude, practical side of the rebel leader is lost sight of in the poet's vision. Marlowe is his own hero, and Tamburlaine is made to utter the deepest secrets of the artist's heart. "What is beauty?" he asks himself.

"If all the pens that ever poets held
Had fed the feeling of their master's thoughts
And every sweetness that inspired their hearts,
Their minds, and muses on admired themes;
If all the heavenly quintessence they still

1. Ellis-Fermor: "Tamburlaine, the Great", page 50.

From their immortal flowers of poesy,
Wherein, as in a mirror, we perceive
The highest reaches of a human wit;
If these had made one poem's period,
And all combined in beauty's worthiness
Yet should there hover in their restless heads
One thought, one grace, one wonder, at the least
Which into words no virtue can digest."

Tamburlaine is a strong and eager-hearted poet and these words are the key to his career. He sees forever an unattainable loveliness beckoning him across the world and how can his ardent blood rest, "attemptless, faint and destitute"?

"Our souls, whose faculties can comprehend
The wondrous architecture of the world
And measure every wandering planet's course
Still climbing after knowledge infinite
And always moving as the restless spheres
Will us to wear ourselves, and never rest,
Until we reach the ripest fruit of all,
That perfect bliss and sole felicity
The sweet fruition of an earthly crown."

The beauty of his captive bride, Zenocrate, 'lovelier than the love of Jove', moves him to rapturous utterance. When she is taken from him by death, he pictures the bliss that awaits her beyond the grave, in lines that with their haunting and impressive refrain, fall upon the ear like a solemn chant:

Now walk the angels on the floor of heaven,
As sentinels to warn the immortal souls,

To entertain divine Zenocrate.
The cherubims and holy seraphims
That sing and play before the King of Kings
Use all their voices and their instruments
To entertain divine Zenocrate.
And in this sweet and curious harmony,
The God that tunes this music to our souls,
Holds out his hand in highest majesty
To entertain divine Zenocrate."

Similarly Tamburlaine rises to lyrism over the show and color of the world. He revels in the thought of sun-bright armor, of milk-white harts drawing ivory sleds, of Turkish carpets beneath the chariot wheels, of a hundred kings or more with 'so many crowns of burnished gold'. Never again till the coming of Keats did the sensuous imagination speak in tones so full and rich. He is fascinated by the vast and mysterious charm of old-world cities, of Bagdad, and Babylon and Samarcand.

" 'And ride in triumph through Persepolis!'
Is it not brave to be a king, Techelles?
Usumcasane and Theridamis,
Is it not passing brave to be a king
'And ride in triumph through Persepolis?' "

That ambition he satisfies to the full. Not only the King of Persia, but the emperor of the Turks, the Soldan of Egypt and a host of minor potentates fall before his victorious arms. Even the deities he claims as tributaries:

'The God of War resigns his room to me,
Meaning to make me general of the world.

Jove, viewing me in arms, looks pale and wan,
Fearing my power shall pull him from his throne:
Wher'er I come the Fatal Sisters sweat
And grisly death, by running to and fro
To do their ceaseless homage to my sword.'

Thus when sickness suddenly strikes him down, in revenge he would carry war against the immortals, who have ventured to dispute his supremacy:

'What daring gods torments my body thus,
And seeks to conquer mighty Tamburlaine?
Come, let us march against the powers of heaven,
And set black streamers in the firmament
To signify the slaughter of the gods.'

He seeks with scornful glance to scare his 'slave, the ugly monster, Death', but the 'villain' still comes stealing back, and at last, he yields with the hard-wrung avowal that 'Tamburlaine, the scourge of God, must die'. Such is Marlowe's first hero, a veritable incarnation of the genius of the Renaissance.

Yet in the second part of the play, the character of Tamburlaine has changed. The poet has begun to see the discrepancy between his dream of the life of action and the world of practical life. There is little exultation; rather, Marlowe seems to be striving to sweep again into the tireless, spontaneous rhythms of the first part. But the Tamburlaine of the second part gains in humanity. That he is capable of breaking down in his grief brings him humanly nearer to our understanding than the invincible visionary of the first part.

The same is true of the other characters. When Tamburlaine ceases to blind us with his splendor, we can see them more accurately

in their true light, not as figures in the background, but as potential centres of drama. Zenocrate, who is allowed only one effective speech in the first part, emerges in the second part as a powerfully moving figure who commands Tamburlaine himself when she lies on her death-bed:

'I fare, my Lord, as other Empresses
That when this fraile and transitory flesh
Hath sucked the measure of that vitall aire
That feeds the body with his dated health
Wanes with enforst and necessary change.'

These are not words that would appeal to the Tamburlaine who held 'the Fates fast bound in iron chains', but it is not the same Tamburlaine, but one who can cry:

'If thou pittiest Tamburlaine the great
Come down from heaven and live with me againe.'

And again, 'Though she be dead, yet let me think she lives'. It is Theridamis, who has followed him through the conquest of the world, who here gently leads his Lord away: 'This raging cannot make her live'.

In the same way, the minor characters move forward from their subordinate positions and show themselves to have been but obscured by the excess of light upon the central figure; that removed, individuality is revealed in them. Theridamis attempts his conquest of Olympia; Calyphas makes his gallant and humorous protest against the Scythian cult of arms.

Instead of interpreting events in their full meaning, Marlowe approached his subject with a preconceived law of his own and accepted from the material only such parts as confirmed it. He deliber-

ately turns aside from the consideration of the desolation and ruin that follow Tamburlaine's triumphal march. He is unable to include in one poetic concept the desire of Tamburlaine 'Lift upward and divine' and the fate of Bajazet 'So great, so powerful .... and that night a slave.' Unable to see the glories of the conquered and the conqueror in the same world, he strips Bajazet of his valor and dignity to make his central figure shine the greater.

His method brings with it artistic defects. The play has no dramatic unity; the scenes are held together by the dominating personality of the central figure, and apart from him, they would fall asunder like a house of cards. Whereas Shakespeare in "Macbeth" shows the working out of the destiny that attends upon an over-reaching ambition, Marlowe is sympathetic with ambition and no avenging ghosts dog the footsteps of Tamburlaine. He simply continues his wild career till the weapons of war fall from his nerveless hands, and when he lies dead, his eldest son recites over his bier an epitaph suitable for the most virtuous of men:

'Let earth and heaven his timeless death deplore,
For both their worths will equal him no more.'

But what lifts this play above the many that glorify conquest and power is the element of poetic vision which is present in the play. For Marlowe saw in Tamburlaine a vision and aspiration fraught with hitherto unimagined significance. To explore the soul of Tamburlaine became one with exploring the soul of his own 'desires, lift upward and divine'. The illumination and splendor haloed about the figure and background of Tamburlaine come, then, not from the story, (for Marlowe was gloriously mistaken in Timur) but from the world of the poet's imagination.

It is when this spirit has departed from the play, as it does in the second part that the story of Tamburlaine becomes a story of conquest, rapine, bloodshed and violence. Tamburlaine becomes the Timur Khan of the historians.

The dominant trait in Marlowe's genius is its youthfulness; and we approach nowhere else so near to the essential character of the poet as in these two early plays, which, if they did not actually begin his career of authorship, certainly introduced him first to public notice. It remains an open question whether the gain in form and objectivity in the later dramas brings with it a sufficient compensation for the decrease in boyish ideality.

After "Tamburlaine" there could be no question of any continuation of the Religious or Classical Drama. Both were routed, and still more important, the 'jigging veins' and the 'conceits of clownage' were likewise swept to one side.

XI. THE TRAGICALL HISTORY OF DOCTOR FAUSTUS

A. Source

From the exploits of Tamburlaine, Marlowe turned to a subject of a very different kind, but one peculiarly suited to his genius. The legend of a man who sells his soul to the devil seems to have appeared about the sixth century and to have come down the Middle Ages in many forms; in one form it was used by Calderon in "El Magico Prodigioso". In the early part of the 16th century, it became identified with a Dactor Faustus, who practiced necromancy, and was the friend of Paracelsus and Cornelius Agrippa. Conrad Muth, the human-

ist, came across a magician at Erfurt called Georgius Faustus Hemitheus of Heidelburg. Trithemius, in 1506, found a Faustus who boasted that if all the works of Plato and Aristotle were burnt, he could restore them from memory. Melancthon knew a Johannes Faustus born at Knutlingen,,in Wurtemberg, not far from his own home, who studied magic at Cracow, and afterwards "roamed about and talked of secret things".

The first literary version of the Faustus story was the "Volksbuch", which, published by Spiess in 1587, at Frankfort-on-the-Main, soon after appeared in England as "The History of the Damnable Life and Deserved Death of Dr. John Faustus". To this translation of the Faustus book, Marlowe generally adhered; that is to say, in the incidents of the drama, and their sequence, he followed his authority. The wearisome comic scenes, which Marlowe may or may not have written are copied with special fidelity. Marlowe's play was probably the first dramatization of the Faust legend; it became immediately popular, not only in England, but abroad. "Doctor Faustus", as well as "The Jew of Malta" was acted in German by an English company in 1608, during the Carnival at Graetz, and remained a favorite at Vienna throughout the 17th and 18th centuries.

B. Date

The position of "Doctor Faustus" as the immediate successor of "Tamburlaine" in the series of Marlowe's works is well established by the testimony of metre and dramatic structure. External evidence verifies the conclusions of literary criticism and points with some certainty to the winter of 1588/9 as the date of the play's completion. The allusion to the 'fiery keele at Antwerpe's bridge'(1,124) and to the Duke of Parma as oppressor of the Netherlands(1121) de-

termine the extreme limits of composition - 1585 and 1590, respectively.

The hero was played by Alleyn, who also created the part of "Tamburlaine". The play went through numerous editions in book form, of which the earliest extant is the Quarto of 1604, republished with very slight changes in 1609. There is a later version considerably altered and expanded, belonging to the year 1616, and undoubtedly incorporating work by other hands, though also possibly preserving portions of Marlowe's original work omitted in the 1604 Quarto. Thus here as in the case of "Tamburlaine", we are entitled to recognize the broad fact that Marlowe is not to be held responsible for all the weaker elements in the play, as we know it; but there is no safe criterion by which we can definitely reject scenes as unauthenic.

C. Criticism

Of all Marlowe's plays, "Doctor Faustus" is of most interest to-day for it can be revived and hold the attention of the modern audience. The first dramatic employment of the Faust legend, which was later to be made by Goethe into the classic dramatic poem of the questing intellect, it illustrates the quaint mixture of superstition and defiant rationalism so characteristic of the Renaissance man-emerging.

Marlowe's treatment of the theme is important. While Faustus in "Volksbuch", Marlowe's Faustus and Goethe's Faust all represent love of knowledge to such a degree that a contract is signed with the powers of evil, yet the Faust of "Volksbuch" is a mere enchanter and the hero of Goethe's masterpiece, though he covets forbidden lore, is at heart a sceptic, who sells himself to the spirit of evil

and, under its guidance, plunges into sensual pleasures. Goethe was compelled to treat magic and Hell with irony. Marlowe's Faustus, on the other hand, revealing the conflicting stress of new and old, remains the chief artistic embodiment of an intellectual attitude dominant at the Renaissance. The Faustus has the genuine Renaissance passion for 'knowledge infinite', but it is not with him as with Browning's Paracelsus, a purely intellectual yearning. He aspires to unlawful knowledge because it is an instrument of power. The sinner becomes a hero, a Tamburlaine, no longer eager to 'ride in triumph through Persepolis', who, at the thought of vaster delights, has ceased to care for the finite splendors of an earthly crown.

"A god is not so glorious as a king,
I think the pleasures they enjoy in Heaven
Cannot compare with kingly joys on earth,"

once declared Tamburlaine's follower, Theridamis. Faustus, thinks otherwise:

"Emperors and kings
Are but obeyed in their several provinces;
Nor can they raise the wind or rend the clouds;
But his dominion that exceeds in this
Stretcheth as far as doth the mind of man;
A sound magician is a demigod."

In the opening scene Faustus is discovered in his study. He discusses each of the arts in turn: Logic, Physic, Law, and Divinity; he has mastered them all, and yet they leave him 'still but Faustus and a man'. He chafes at these mortal limitations and he seeks freedom from them in magic:

'These metaphysics of magicians

And necromantic books aree heavenly.'

These alome promise him 'a world of profit and delight', the command 'of all things that move between the quiet poles', a power exceeding that of kings and emperors. It is thus the passion for omnipotence rather than omniscience that urges Faustus to summon Mephistophilis by incantations to his side.

By bringing an infernal spirit upon the stage, Marlowe was confronted with the difficult problem of presenting the supernatural in visible form. The crude realism of the miracle plays was no longer possible; yet hell had not become refined away from him, as with Goethe into an idea. Marlowe's presentation avoids physical horrors, while retaining a vivid force. This is a remarkable characteristic of his work. "His raptures were all air and fire". In nothing has he shown himself so much the child of the Renaissance as in this repugnance to touch images of physical ugliness. Perondinus insists upon Tamburlaine's lameness, of which Marlowe says no word. The "Volksbuch" is crammed with details concerning the mediaevel Hell; Marlowe's conception of Hell is loftier than Dante's or Milton's. In reply to the question of Faustus:

"How comes it then that thou art out of Hell?"

Mephistophilis replies:

"Why this is Hell, nor am I out of it.
Think"st thou that I who saw the face of God
And tasted the eternal joys of Heaven
Am not tormented with ten thousand Hells,
In being deprived of everlasting bliss?"

Such reticence as this was entirely out of the line of dramatic tradition and even the able revisers of the edition of the play published in 1616 contrived to bring in plenty of horrors, not only in the account of the death of Faustus, but as a description of Hell. Too, Marlowe's point of view is modern, not mediaevel, and the expression is direct, eloquent and passionate, and except for being cast in heroic verse might be the expression of a modern.

Marlowe's Mephistophilis is not the arch-enemy himself, but an attendant spirit upon Lucifer. He is a fallen angel, eager for the prize of 'a glorious soul' and yet sorrowing with a stately pathos over the bliss that he has lost. In his answers to Faustus, there rings the piercing note of a deeper than human despair:

Faust. And what are you that live with Lucifer?
Meph. Unhappy spirits that fell with Lucifer,
Conspired against our God with Lucifer,
And are forever damned with Lucifer.

But this utterance of spiritual agony leaves Faustus unmoved, and he offers to surrender his soul to Lucifer, if he is allowed to live 'four and twenty years in all voluptuousness' with Mephistophilis as his attendant. Here his motive seems to take a lower and more sensual form, but he immediately afterwards reverts to the idea of power in his declaration that by infernal aid he will be 'great emperor of the world'.

Through the play, however, there runs the feeling, of which there is no hint in "Tamburlaine", that the unlawful satisfactions of desire are sinful, and the poet vividly paints the struggles ~~the~~ in Faustus' soul before he finally surrenders himself to the powers of darkness. Good and evil angels whisper their counsel to him, a voice

sounds in his ears: "Abjure this magic, turn to God again". But the temptation is too strong and at midnight in his study alone with Mephistophilis, he seals his bond with blood. The language of his speeches lifts the situation, even to-day, into dignity and tragic interest. The scene is weirdly impressive, for the blood congeals, and Mephistophilis brings coals to melt the blood for Faustus to write. He completes the document in legal wording, and then sees on his arm the mysterious message "Homo, fuge", and Mephistophilis has to divert his thoughts with a pageant of devils who make rich offerings to him. The contract executed, Faustus is bidden ask what he will and he immediately reverts to his old question of the whereabouts of hell. Mephistophilis answers in the same spirit as before:

'Hell hath no limit nor is circumscribed
In one self place: for where we are is hell
And where hell is there must we ever be
And to conclude, when all the world dissolves
And every creature shall be purified,
All places shall be hell that is not heaven.

Faustus then puts his powers to new proof by demanding a wife, the 'fairest maid in Germany'; all his requests are granted by Mephistophilis. Yet Faustus is still troubled by his conscience: the Good Angel keeps whispering 'repent' in his ear, and in an outburst of remorse, he calls upon Christ to save his soul. Hereupon Lucifer rushes in with his cohorts to put an end to such appeals, warning Faustus he is breaking his contract. Faustus, in terror, then vows:

'Never to look to heaven,
Never to name God, or to pray to Him.
To burn His scriptures, to slay His ministers.'

Up to this point the plot has developed on natural and impressive lines, but here it is suddenly arrested. The conjuring tricks which Faustus performs at the courts of the Pope, the German Emperor and the Duke of Vanholt, are out of keeping with the dignity of the true theme of the play.

It would be difficult to name in English literature scenes at all comparable in beauty and power with the famous scene in which Faustus calls up the vision of Helen and the last scene of all. The immortal lines that begin

> 'Is this the face that launched a thousand ships
> And burned the topless towers of Ilium?
> Helen, make me immortal with a kiss.'

have sung forever since in the memories of our race, and when first spoken on the stage must have subdued that Elizabethan audience with their loveliness and evoked, as no speech yet heard in the English theatre had ever done, the exact mood the dramatist desired.

The prose dialogue on the fatal evening when the Doctor's agonized outbursts move his scholars to such touching solicitude, leads up to the highly wrought blank verse soliloquy of Faustus as he is left alone with but one bare hour to live. We thrill at the impassioned beauty, the tragic power of the verse, the gradual mounting of passion and terror. In the frenzy of despair, Faustus appeals to the sun, 'to rise again and make perpetual day'; he seeks to leap up and catch 'one drop' of the blood of Christ; he calls upon the hills to hide him from the heavy wrath of God, upon the earth to gape and harbor him. But the minutes pass and the clock strikes the half-hour. It is too late to hope for mercy; all he now craves is some end to his pain:

'Let Faustus live in hell a thousand years
A hundred thousand, and, at last, be saved.'

And as he curses the immortality that ensures his everlasting torment, the midnight hour strikes and the devils come for their prey. The horrors of hell hedge him in on every side; he gasps out broken agonized prayers for mercy:

'My God, my God! look not so fierce on me!
Adders and serpents, let me breathe awhile!
Ugly Hell, gape not! come not, Lucifer!
I'll burn my books! Ah, Mephistophilis.'

"Exeunt Devils, with Faustus" - and then the Chorus speaks the Epilogue:

'Cut is the branch that might have grown full straight,
And burned is Apollo's laurel bough ---'

poetry again, in the lofty mood the audience must have felt at the moment, closing the drama with the deep voice of beauty. Thus Horatio speaks the epilogue after Hamlet's death, beginning -

'Good night, sweet Prince,
And flights of angels sing thee to thy rest ---'

And who shall say that Shakespeare did not learn that magic creation of a mood, that tragic touch of beauty to round out his play, from Christopher Marlowe?

At first this play seems structurally feeble - merely a string of episodes taken from the old legend. It is in the selection of serious incidents from the prose narrative that Marlowe's genius for the tragic poetry of intense emotion is especially revealed. The play disregards the probabilities in the development of many scenes; the comic interludes are pretty poor stuff (some of them perhaps

from a later hand) and hardly anyone in the play except Faustus makes an impression on our imaginations or sympathies. Yet the play must have had a novel fascination because of its theme and for any audience the character of Faustus himself and the dominance of his soul struggle, so eloquently expressed, give the drama a unity, a compelling atmosphere and mood which compensate for many faults. Moreover, Marlowe was striving for a double effect - he was striving to tell a story interesting to the London mob, and likewise to depict something almost if not quite new on the British stage, the tragedy of a spirit at war with itself. Omit the comic relief in which Faustus does not appear and you have a kind of monologue play that bears more than a fanciful resemblance to Eugene O'Neill's "Emperor Jones". Goethe said of it, "How greatly it is all planned!" Can it be that Goethe is right in spite of the fact that critics of drama have called it a careless string of episodes?

Far more than many of the critics realize the play was probably very cleverly written to please the London populace and also to earn Marlowe's claim to immortality. Marlowe's poetic gift laid the real emphasis not on mere story, but on the deeper places of drama, the human conscience. It marked progress by proving that great drama has a higher mission than story telling. For Marlowe's stately line was poetry, consciously and skilfully used to depict human character, and to create an emotional reaction in an audience. It was a contribution to English drama that made possible many of the great advances of the ensuing decades.

XII. THE JEW OF MALTA

The source of the drama is unknown, and its date cannot be accurately fixed, though it must have been later than the death of the Duke of Guise in December, 1588, mentioned in the Prologue. This prologue is spoken by the spirit of Machiavel, which is supposed to brood over the tragedy, and whose example inspires the actions of Barabas. In Barabas, Marlowe found another of those impassioned figures to which his genius was specially drawn. The opening scene, in which the Jew is found in his counting-house, with heaps of gold before him, is exceedingly powerful and impressive. Only Milton, as Swinburne said, has surpassed it.

As Barabas fingers the coins and hovers over his precious jewels; as he follows imaginatively his argosies 'laden with silk and spice', his avarice ceases to be sordid, and swells to the proportions of a passion for the infinite, though it be only for 'infinite riches in a little room'. Thus there is in Barabas a vein of idealism lacking in the more miserly Shylock of Shakespeare, of whom he is certainly in part the progenitor. Accumulating a treasury of riches is to Barabas sanctified by divine powers:

'Thus trowls our fortune in by land and sea,
And thus we are on every side enriched;
These are the blessings promised to the Jews,
And herein was old Abram's happiness.
What more may heaven do for earthly man
Than thus to pour out plenty in their laps,
Ripping the bowels of the earth for them,
Making the sea their servants, and the winds
To drive their substance with successful blasts?'

Thus when he loses his fortune at one blow, he arouses our sympathy, and we even condone the strategy he uses to regain his wealth. The relations of Abigail to her father probably suggested those of Jessica and Shylock, but Marlowe's heroine certainly has the advantage over Shakespeare's in filial loyalty. Like Jessica she has given her heart to a Christian lover, but Barabas craftily brings about his death at the hands of a rival, whereupon she again retires to the convent though no longer in the spirit of hypocrisy.

From this point on the play declines, and the large conception of the Jew topples over into harsh and extravagant caricature. The poet's genius may have faltered in its flight, or he may have worked hastily to complete the work by a certain date, or it may have been finished by a collaborator. Professor Tucker-Brooke thinks the latter is unlikely, for he sees "little reason to believe that the poet's general design has anywhere been very seriously tampered with, and to the very end of the play there occur, among obvious corruptions, verses which it seems all but impossible to deny to Marlowe."[1]

When Shakespeare a few years later, took up the same subject, the"Merchant of Venice" by force of his sweetness, humanity and humor, easily rises to a higher pitch of art. Certainly Marlowe's play gives no hint of the complex glories of "The Merchant of Venice". "The Jew of Malta" shows the transition between Marlowe,the youthful poet, with his intense and fascinating personality, and Marlowe, the mature dramatist.

1 Marlowe, C.:Works, ed. by C.F. Tucker Brooke, page 233.

XIII. Edward II.

A. Source

Marlowe's authorities were the chronicles of Fabian, Stow and Holinshed, but he selected the material for his tragedy with the imaginative freedom characteristic of Shakespeare's use of the same sources. Chronological accuracy is not attempted, but the true meaning of history is faithfully represented.

B. Authorship

Marlowe's name appears on the title-pages of all the early editions of this drama and has never been questioned. Publication followed so closely upon the writing that there is no reason for suspecting the presence of alien matter, and the text is probably purer than that of any other of Marlowe's dramatic works.

C. Date

"Edward II" is generally agreed to be the maturest and, with the possible exception of "The Massacre of Paris", the latest of Marlowe's plays. There is, however, very little external evidence by which to determine the precise year of composition.

On July 6, 1593, William Jones registered the play under the title: "A booke Intituled 'The Troublesome Reign and Lamentable Death of Edward the Second, king of England, with the tragicall fall of proud Mortymer'". The title-page of the 1593 edition also stated that the play had been 'sondry times publiquely acted in the honorable Citie of London, By the right honorable the Earle of Pembroke his Seruantes'. No doubt the play was well-known on the stage before it was printed; probably then the year 1591, or the early part of 1592, saw the completion of "Edward II" and its presentation on the stage.

D. Criticism

In this work Marlowe entered upon a new field. Turning aside from the fortunes of foreign and semi-legendary personages like Tamburlaine, Faustus and Barabas, he went to the national history of his country and, in doing so, created the first genuine historical play. By common consent, this play is recognized as being, after Shakespeare's, the finest specimen of the English historical drama, while, in regard to its predecessors, it has the advantage of being anterior to all of them in date of its production. It is in this play that Marlowe's powers as a dramatist are at their highest.

In the matter of plot and construction, "Edward II" stands on a different level from any of Marlowe's previous works. Instead of being a collection of unconnected episodes, it is a complex and organic whole, working up gradually step by step to a singularly powerful climax. In style, too, it marks an advance. The 'high astounding terms' of the earlier period have almost entirely disappeared; the play is full of sober strength, very different from the Titanic force that overflowed in "Tamburlaine". 'The measure', as has been well said, 'that had thundered the threats of Tamburlaine' is made now 'to falter the sobs of a broken heart.'

However, it is in the powers of characterization that the play shows most distinctive evidences of growth. In contrast to Marlowe's earlier dramas where each is dominated by the commanding figure of the hero, which overshadows and dwarfs the other people in the play, here the characters stand out in bold relief; their motives are not in question, and the events of the drama are made to flow naturally from one central cause. The whole action of "Edward II" turns on the King's abuse of his power. Edward has no sense of the difficul-

ties of his position; he resolutely shuts his eyes to the harshness of facts. He is a king and will suffer no limitation of his prerogative - "Am I a king, and must be overruled?" - is his perpetual reply to all objections, and this point, emphasized at the beginning, is never lost sight of.

While the king stands out as the central character, the figures of Mortimer and Gaveston are particularly well-defined, also. Gaveston, the favorite, is portrayed with much insight and skill. He has a Frenchman's dislike for London and Londoners, and a contempt for the English nobles whom he infuriates with his foreign airs. As Mortimer indignantly complains:

'I have not seen a dapper Jack so brisk;
He wears a short Italian hooded cloak,
Loaded with pearl, and, in his Tuscan cap,
A jewel of more value than the crown.
While others walk below, the king and he
From out a window laugh at such as we,
And flout out train, and jest at our attire.'

He craftily strengthens his hold on the king's affections by administering to his artistic and musical tastes and providing him with congenial entertainment. So successful are his plans that for his sake Edward proves false to his duties as a king and a husband. He leaves his wife to pine with grief at his neglect of her, and offers to share his kingdom amongst the lords if they will allow him to have some corner left to frolic with his 'dearest Gaveston'. The nobles and clergy compel the favorite's banishment for a time, but he is quickly recalled, only to exhibit the same insolent spirit as before, bidding the 'base, leaden earls to go home and eat their tenant's beef.'

They answer the taunt by rising in revolt. Gaveston is captured and sentenced to die.

When he is gone, his place is taken by Young Spencer, who, though more slightly drawn, is skilfully discriminated from Gaveston by a few firm and vigorous touches. He is lacking in the defiant gaiety of the Frenchman, but he outrivals him in cynical audacity and statecraft, and in the end, he draws down upon himself a similar fate.

At the head of the barons in their conflict with the favorites stands Mortimer, who is portrayed with great spirit and power. Mortimer resembles Marlowe's former heroes, somewhat, particularly Tamburlaine. The lines of his character are, of course, toned down to suit the different environment, but there is the same note of aspiring ambition. It is he who throughout is the advocate of violent measures, urging the barons to 'parley' only with their naked swords. He is eager to depose the king unless he consents to banish Gaveston, and when the favorite on his return provokes him by his insolence, Mortimer stabs him. When taken prisoner in an unsuccessful revolt and condemned to the Tower, his haughty spirit chafes at such a curb on his 'virtue that aspires to heaven'. He escapes to France and there gains the love of Isabel, the Queen, with whom he returns to England. Having overthrown Edward, he vaunts his authority with tyrannical arrogance; it is here that he most resembles Tamburlaine, for he speaks as one who makes fortune's wheel turn as he please:

'The prince I rule, the queen do I command,
And with a lowly congé to the ground
The proudest lords salute me as I pass;
I seal, I cancel, I do what I will.'

Fearing an uprising in favor of the king, he procures the removal of Edward to Berkeley Castle, where the brutal assassination is carried out. However, when the young Edward overthrows Mortimer, the latter meets his fate with a haughty indifference and without a touch of regret. He has made the most of this life and he looks forward with zest to the possibilities in the next:

'Base Fortune, now I see, that in thy wheel
There is a point, to which when men aspire
They tumble headlong down: that point I touched,
And seeing there was no place to mount up higher,
Why should I grieve at my declining fall?
Farewell, fair queen; weep not for Mortimer,
That scorns the world, and, as a traveller,
Goes to discover countries yet unknown.'

Thus here at the close of Marlowe's last play, the note is struck that rings throughout his writings - contempt for human, earthly limitations and a yearning to fulfill all one's desires to the utmost, to a completeness that is denied on this earth.

There is one quite weak point in the play and that is the portrayal of the Queen. She is drawn more elaborately than any of the poet's other women characters, yet she fails to arouse sympathetic interest. Some of the scenes where the Queen is present are admirable; for instance, the reconciliation between her and the King(ActI, iv, 320-40) is treated lightly and delicately. But her transition to the side of Mortimer is crudely handled, and her ready consent to her husband's destruction is pretty callous.

The career of "Edward II" seems an ironical retort to Tamburlaine's exultant cry,"Is it not brave to be a king?". Throughout the

earlier scenes of the drama, he exhibits every form of royal baseness. It is only with his fall that he begins to appeal to our sympathies. It is certain that 'the reluctant pangs of abdicating royalty' (to quote Lamb's famous phrase) has never been more finely portrayed than in the closing scenes of the drama. In the superb climax of the last dread scene in Berkeley Castle, the poet's genius has achieved its highest triumph in combining with extreme and even painful realism the poetic touch that keeps everything within the limits of true art. What more pathetic lines than

> 'Tell Isabel, the queen, I looked not thus,
> When for her sake I ran at tilt in France,
> And there unhorsed the Duke of Clermont.'

In vain, he pleads to the murderer for his life, and too weak to resist, is barbarously done to death.

Hazlitt pronounces the death scene to be "certainly superior" to the parallel scene in "Richard II" and "in heart-breaking distress and the sense of human weakness claiming pity from utter helplessness and conscious misery, is not surpassed by any writer whatever."[1] This high praise is more than confirmed by Lamb, who says, "the death scene of Marlowe's King moves pity, and terror beyond any scene, ancient or modern, with which I am acquainted."[2]

However, Shakespeare, in order to show how Richard's downfall is brought about by his own weaknesses, did not intend to awaken a reaction in the King's favor by portraying too vividly his sufferings in prison and death. Marlowe, on the other hand, does just that, and in the sufferings of the last scenes, we forget Edward's faults. Thus Shakespeare's moral point of view is higher than Marlowe's, but

1. Hazlitt, W: English Literature, page 55
2. Lamb, C. : Dramatic Specimens, page 26

as far as closely sustained dramatic interest is concerned, Marlowe's play is without question the superior one.

XIV. THE MASSACRE OF PARIS

The date of this historical piece is unknown, but it cannot have been an early play, as it ends with the death of HenryIII of France, which happened in 1589. On January 30, 1593, the play was performed at Henslowe's theatre by Lord Strange's Company.

Of all the known plays of Marlowe, this one is in its present state much the least meritorious. The play has come down to us in an imperfect form, yet even when complete it must have been Marlowe's poorest work. It is probably the result of a hastily conceived and carelessly worked-out idea. There is nothing to indicate either collaboration or careful revision.

It is chiefly interesting as a reaction of contemporary English feeling upon the Massacre of St. Bartholomew and the events which followed. Marlowe is strongly Protestant here and draws all the Catholic characters in very dark colors. Henry III, the suitor of Queen Elizabeth, is given fairer treatment. The most powerfully drawn figure is the Duke of Guise, who too may be counted among Marlowe's aspiring, ambitious characters. His character and purposes are frankly revealed in a notable soliloquy:

'That like I best, that flies beyond my reach
Set me to scale the high Pyramides
And thereon set the diadem of France:
I'll either rend it with my nails to nought,

Or mount the top with my aspiring wings,

Although my downfall be the deepest hell.'

Guise reminds one of Mortimer, and in the general theme of the play - the struggle between a feeble king and rebellious nobles - this work is an echo or a weak anticipation of "Edward II".

XV. THE TRAGEDIE OF DIDO, QUEENE OF CARTHAGE

A. Source

Of more interest is"Dido", published the year after Marlowe's death, in 1594. It is a dramatic version of the first, second, and fourth books of the Aeneid. The Latin text, eight lines of which are woven directly into the last act, has evidently been used. Marlowe is not indebted to English translations or paraphrases. Large portions of the play are closely translated from the corresponding passages of Virgil, but the rendering is marked by ease and grace. The chief additions to Virgil's story are: The Prelude (I,i,1-49), the great elaboration of the part of Iarbus, with Anna's love for him and the suicide of both at the end; the details about Dido's suitors and about the riggings of the ships; a much more complicated treatment of the confusion of identity between Ascanius and Cupid; the double use of the episode of Mercury's warning to Aeneas, and the unsuccessful first effort of the hero to sail to Italy.

B. Date and Authorship

The title-page of this tragedy states that it was played by the Children of Her Majesty's Chapel and written by Christopher

Marlowe and Thomas Nash. The connection of Thomas Nash with the play is uncertain and on the evidence of style would appear to be very slight. There is hardly any resemblance between Nash's only other extant dramatic work, "Summer's Last Will and Testament", and any part of "Dido", whereas the peculiar style of Marlowe can be recognized in almost every scene.

In no other case can Marlowe be shown to have collaborated with a fellow-dramatist during his London career, unless with Shakespeare in the Henry VI plays. The conclusion would seem almost unavoidable that "Dido" is the product of an old college partnership between two Cambridge friends. Probably Nash was in some way connected with the play after 1587. Nash may have prepared it for production by the Chapel Children, or for publication after that event. This is probably the same "Dido" which the Lord Admiral's Company, under the auspices of Henslowe, acted for the first time on January 8, 1597-8.

C. Editions

The early texts of Marlowe are in most cases rare, and "Dido" is the rarest of them all. It appeared in print only once between its composition and 1825. This sole source for the text is a Quarto printed by the Widow Orwin for Thomas Woodcocke in 1594. The Restoration bookseller, Francis Kirkman, presumably possessed a copy of this Quarto, for he lists "Dido, Queen of Carthage", by Marlowe and Nash, in his catalogues of 1661 and 1671. Langbaine mentioned it as a work he had never seen (1691), and Malone, at the close of the 18th century, called it 'one of the scarcest plays in the English language'. Only three copies can at present be found. These are (1) the Bodleian copy, in the Bodleian Library; (2) the Folger copy, now in the possession of Mr. H.C. Folger of New York; (3) the

Huntington copy, in the Henry E. Huntington Library, San Marino, California.

Apparently at one time there was another copy of inestimable value. In a posthumous work of 1748, Bishop Thomas Tanner (1674-1735) refers definitely to an 'elegiac song' on the untimeliness of Marlowe's death by Thomas Nash, which he says was prefixed to the play "Dido". Thomas Warton, in the third volume of his "History of English Poetry" (1781, page 435) has a footnote: 'Nash, in his Elegy prefixed to Marlowe's "Dido" mentions five of his plays'. Shortly after, the scholar Malone wrote to Warton for more specific information and received the following reply: 'He informed me by letter that a copy of this play was in Osborne's catalogue in the year, 1754; that he then saw it in his shop (together with several of Mr. Oldys's books that Osborne had purchased) & that the elegy in question "on Marlowe's untimely death" was inserted immediately after the title-page; that it mentioned a play of Marlowe's entitled "The Duke of Guise" and four others; but whether particularly by name, he could not recollect. Unluckily he did not purchase this rare piece & it is now God knows where.'

This copy is still missing and, since Warton, no one has apparently seen it. The elegy was probably printed on a leaf inserted between the title-page and the first page of text.

D. Criticism

Many word-patterns and mental pictures for which Marlowe is famous appear to have had their first expression in "Dido". They are found most often in "Tamburlaine" and the translation of Ovid's Elegies, but some of the most striking link this play with such late works as "Edward II" and "Hero and Leander". Very likely, Marlowe subjected this play to complete revision at the time he was writing the later

plays.

"Dido": Yet flung I forth, and desperate of my life, (L.505 ff.)
Ran in the thickest throngs, and with this sword
Sent many of their sauadge ghosts to hell.

"Tam.": But then run desperate through the thickest throngs,(L.3329)

"Dido": And clad her in a Chrystall liuerie, (L. 1414)

"Tam.": And cloath it in a christall liuerie, (L. 2573)

"Dido": Doe thou but smile, and clowdie heauen will cleare, (L.155)

"Tam.": That with thy lookes canst cleare the darkened Sky: (L.1220)
Whose chearful looks do cleare the clowdy aire (L.2572)

"Dido": For in his looks I see eternitie (L. 1328ff)
And heele make me immortal with a kisse

"Faustus": Sweet Helen, make me immortal with a kisse (L. 1330)
Here will I dwell, for Heaven be in those lips. (L.1333)

"Dido": So thou wouldst proue as true as Paris did, (L.1554-6)
Would, as faire Troy was, Carthage might be sackt,
And I be calde a second Helena.

"Faustus": And all is drosse that is not Helena: (L.1334-6)
I wil be Paris, and for loue of thee,
Insteede of Troy shal Wertenberge be sackt.

"Dido": Threatning a thousand deaths at euery glaunce. (L.526)

H.&L.: Threatning a thousand deaths at euerie glaunce. (L.382)

"Dido": And let rich Carthage fleete upon the seas, (L.1340)

"Ed,II": This Ile shall fleete upon the Ocean (L.344)

"Dido": And thou Aeneas, Dido's treasurie (L.725-7)
In whose faire bosome I will looke more wealth

"Ed.II": No other iewels hang about my neck (L.628-30)
Then these my lord, nor let me haue more wealth
Then I may fetch from this ritch treasurie

The above are but a few of the repetitions of favorite lines or phrases found in his plays.

Dido, unlike the complex Cleopatra of Shakespeare, is yet another of Marlowe's embodiments of limitless desire, which in her case takes the form of a great passion. Drawn with power and refinement, Marlowe succeeds in making her attractive despite the fact she is the ardent pursuer of the love of Aeneas. She rises to lyrical ecstacy when she finds that her love is returned:

> 'What more than Delian music do I hear,
> That calls my soul from forth his living seat,
> To move unto the measure of delight? ...
> Heaven envious of our joys is waxen pale,
> And when we whisper, then the stars fall down
> To be partakers of our honey talk.'

When Aeneas sails away from Carthage, she cries that she will follow him:

> 'I'll frame me wings of wax, like Icarus,
> And o'er his ship will soar unto the sun,
> That they may melt, and I fall in his arms.'

In despair, she commits suicide, followed immediately by faithful Anna and Iarbas. The latter, drawn with some force, is rather interesting as the jealous rival of Aeneas. Aeneas is not very colorful, being notable chiefly for his account of the fall of Troy.

"The most useful aesthetic criticism is therefore not that which concerns the total effect conveyed by this work of borrowed plot and rather composite style, but that which deals with the many illuminating individual passages where we see the impact of Vergil's splendid gravity upon the most exuberantly romantic of the Elizabeth-

an dramatists, or mark the blend of ardent impulse with austere intellectual insight that best defines Marlowe's view of life."[1]

XVI. HERO AND LEANDER

We turn now to the consideration of Marlowe's narrative poem, "Hero and Leander", probably the latest of Marlowe's writings. Left a fragment at his death, it was licensed a few months later, September 28, 1593) by John Wolf. The earliest known edition to exist was that published by Edward Blount in 1598. This edition contained only Marlowe's portion without Chapman's arguments and divisions into sestiads.

The popularity of the poem with the Elizabethan public must have been enormous, for the literature of the time abounds in allusions to it, and the list of early editions is a most impressive one. There were probably three separate ones in 1598, others in 1600, 1606, 1609, 1613, 1616, 1617, 1622, 1629 and 1637.

Lines 183-198 of the third sestiad seem to indicate that Chapman concluded the poem by request of Marlowe, though such an interpretation may be a straining of the vague hints in those lines in question. In 1598, there was published another attempt at completing the poem. This work, by Henry Petowe, is considered of little poetic value.

Drawing his subject from the Greek poem ascribed to Musaeus, he enriches it with luxurious additions, which not only give a new character to the piece, but expand it considerably beyond the scope or the design of the original. Little more is taken from Musaeus than the story. The poetry and passionate descriptions belong to Marlowe.

1. Tucker-Brooke, C.F.:The Tragedy of Dido", page 253.

'The brightest flower of the English Renaissance', it bears Marlowe's intensely personal impression. Without it, we would never have known the full sweetness and range of his genius. It has been said that for sustained beauty and consummate workmanship, it is the most perfect product of his pen. It is a free and fresh and eager song, "drunk with gladness", full of ideal beauty that finds its expression in the form and color of things, above all, in the bodies of men and women. No Elizabethan had so keen a sense of physical loveliness as these lines reveal:

'His body was straight as Circe's wand
Ioue might haue sipt out Nectar from his hand.
Euen as delicious meat is to the tast,
So was his necke in touching, and surpast
The white of Pelop's shoulder. I could tell ye
How smooth his brest was, & how white his bellie,
And whose immortall fingars did imprint
That heauenly path, with many a curious dint,
That runs along his backe, ...'

The atmosphere of the poem is highly sensuous, but the tale moves forward with such lightness and freedom, and Marlowe's imaginative touch is so unerring, that there is never a feeling of closeness. We turn aside from the close and sensual atmosphere of Shakespeare's "Venus and Adonis" to the free and open air, the color and light, the swift and various music of Marlowe's poem.

Shelley has scarcely surpassed the sweet gravity of which our "elder Shelley" here reaches:

'It lies not in our powers to love or hate,
For will in us is overruled by fate.

When two are stript long ere the course begin
We wish that one should loose, the other win;
And one especially do we affect
Of two gold Ingots like in each respect.
The reason no man knowes, let it suffise,
What we behold is censur'd by our eies.
Where both deliberat, the loue is slight,
Who euer lov'd, that lov'd not at first sight?'

Chapman's completion of the poem has been added to every edition except the first. Marlowe apparently intended the poem to be one piece, but Chapman broke it up into sestiads and added a rhyming argument to each. Whether the poem derives any benefit from this is to be doubted, except it serves to show where Marlowe left off, and Chapman began.

In tone, there is no resemblence between the parts whatever. One immediately feels the difference in passing from the musical flow and choice diction of Marlowe to the rugged verse of Chapman. In places, Chapman's lines show real poetic feeling and grace - notably in the tale of Teras - and though usually obscure, is always profound and vigorous.

No other narrative poem in English literature can equal Marlowe's 800 lines, either in structure or in artistic expression. Here is Marlowe's genius at its best, certainly in its most complete and well-rounded development.

XVII. OVID'S ELEGIES

Marlowe's translations of the Elegies of Ovid survives in at least six early editions, all of which are undated. However, there would seem to be little doubt as to the period of composition of the poems. The work is characterized by a youthful stiffness of expression, by errors in the translating, and awkward metres. It is almost certain the work of his Cambridge period.

Two of the most famous mistranslations are 'Snakes leape by verse from caues of broken mountaines' for 'Carmine dissiliunt, abruptis faucibus, angues', and 'did sing with corne' for 'canebat frugibus'. Some of the translated lines are utterly meaningless, as for example: 'On her white necke but for hurt cheekes be led'.

Though this work is certainly a failure both as poetry and as Latin translation, it does show some promise, for there is a certain enthusiasm and real poetic fervour present that argues well for the future of the youthful poet.

No doubt the work was published without the approval of the authorities, for some years after Marlowe's death, the bishops fixed upon it as a proper sacrifice to be burned by the common hangman. If the object of this was to heap further discredit upon the name of Marlowe, and through him, upon the stage, it ought to be remembered that the publishing of it was none of his doing, and that the ideas are the property of Ovid.

XVIII. THE PASSIONATE SHEPHERD

The best known and one of the most beautiful of Marlowe's compositions, this poem has retained its popularity for over 300 years. It was originally printed (with the exception of the fourth, and sixth stanzas) in the "Passionate Pilgrim", a miscellany of poems by different persons, although first ascribed to Shakespeare. "The Passionate Pilgrim" was published in 1599, and in 1600, the song appeared under Marlowe's name in "England's Helicon". Always immensely popular, the song has been used by many other poets. The music to which the song was sung was discovered by Sir John Hawkins in an Elizabethan manuscript, and is given in Chappell's collection of "National English Airs" and Boswell's edition of Malone's Shakespeare. The name of this earlier song is "Adieu, my dear".

Shakespeare quoted from "The Passionate Shepherd" in "The Merry Wives" (I,iii), and Raleigh, Herrick and Donne have either written an answer to it or have constructed poems using it as a model.

The poem in "England's Helicon" consisted of six stanzas, whereas in "The Passionate Pilgrim", only four had been given. The added stanzas are the fourth and sixth of the 1600 version. In Walton's "Complete Angler" the song has seven stanzas, the added one being inserted between the fifth and sixth of the 1600 edition. It is not known where Walton obtained it.

The poem breathes the true air of the country,,and is addressed by the shepherd lover to his beloved. The pleasures that he promises her are 1.-sitting by the river, watching the shepherds with their flocks and listening to the birds sing to the accompaniment of a waterfall; 2.-rosy-beds and flower-adorned garments; 3 - a lambs-wool gown and gold-buckled slippers; 4- a belt of straw and ivy with coral

clasps and amber studs; 5- entertainments by the shepherds on May mornings. The song ends:

'If these delights thy mind may move,
Then live with me and be my love.'

The imitations of the poem include the formula of invitation or its equivalent, which normally the lover addresses to his mistress; and the catalogue of pleasures which the speaker will provide for her if she accepts. Frequently the imitators use Marlowe's metrical scheme of verse: iambic tetrameters, rhyming in couplets and grouped in stanzas of four verses.

The ultimate source of Marlowe's poem seems to be the "Idyl XI" of Theocritus. Here the Cyclops, Polyphemus, a shepherd courts the nymph, Galatea. In his address to her, he attempts to offset his personal defects and to overcome her repugnance by enumerating his possessions and listing the rustic delicacies and pleasures which she shall enjoy if she but come to him. A formal invitation occurs in the course of the Cyclops' speech. A more immediate classical source for the poem is to be found in Ovid's "Metamorphoses" Book XIII, which also gives a version of the legend of Polyphemus and Galatea.

The earliest employment of the invitation to love in English is by Marlowe himself in his earliest produced play, "Tamburlaine". Tamburlaine courts the captive Princess in much the same manner as Polyphemus with Galatea. Tamburlaine opens his suit with

'Disdaines Zenocrate to liue with me?

He then promises her various luxuries, including an escort of Tartars and rich garments. His army's booty

Shall all we offer to Zenocrate
And then my selfe to faire Zenocrate.

Later on in Part II, Act IV, ii, in the love scene between Theridamis and Olympia, he courts her by telling her of the joys for her if she but consent to be his Queene.

These are more like advance hints than echoes of "The Passionate Shepherd", but in "The Jew of Malta", there is an invitation to love that is so close in its phrasing to the lyric that it seems necessary to regard it as directly reminiscent. Ithimore, the slave of Barabas, exhorts Bellamira, the courtezan, to flee with him to Greece, the rustic beauties of which he extols to her as delights to be enjoyed. The passage begins with an invitation and ends with

'Thou in those Groues, by Dis aboue
Shalt liue with me and be my loue.'

Marlowe may have been parodying himself, or as has been suggested, they may be the work of another dramatist seeking to write in Marlowe's style.

There are at least three passages in "Edward II" that show traces of the influence of the poem: (1) Gaveston's opening soliloquy, where after Gaveston receives the invitation of the King to return to court, he comments

'What greater blisse can hap to Gaueston
Than liue and be the favorit of a king?'

(2) Further on, (L..51-73) Gaveston still soliloquizing, forms plans for maintaining himself in the royal favor. He plans a series of delights suited to the King's tastes; (3) Again, Edward himself borrows from the lyric. In reply to the expostulations of the nobles against his renewed relations with Gaveston, he concludes an angry speech with

'Ile bandie with the Barons and the Earls
And eyther die or liue with Gaveston.'

In "Dido" there are some hints of the lyric. First there is the wooing of Ganymede by Jupiter, who promises him celestial pleasures in return for his love. In Act II Venus bribes Ascanius to remain with her while Cupid, as Ascanius, fires Dido with love for Aeneas. She promises such gifts as would appeal to a child. Later in the play, Dido begs Aeneas to remain with her in Carthage

'Conditionally that thou wilt stay with me.'

and she promises him wondrous gifts. In Act IV Cupid as Ascanius, is the object of the love of the nurse, who promises him special joys if he will go with her.

There are in all fourteen passages in Marlowe's plays in which the lyric is suggested.

Come liue with mee, and be my loue,
And we will all the pleasures proue,
That Vallies, groues, hills and fields,
Woods, or steepie mountaine yeeldes.

And wee will sit upon the Rocks,
Seeing the Sheepheards feede theyr flocks
By shallow Riuers, to whose falls
Melodious byrds sings Madrigalls.

And I will make thee beds of Roses,
And a thousand fragrant poesies,
A cap of flowers, and a kirtle,
Imbroydred all with leaues of Mirtle.

A gowne made of the finest wooll,
Which from our pretty Lambes we pull,
Fayre lined slippers for the cold,
With buckles of the purest gold.

A belt of straw and Iuie buds,
With Corall clasps and Amber studs,
And if these pleasures may thee moue,
Come liue with me, and be my loue.

The Sheepheards Swaines shall daunce & sing
For thy delight each May-morning
If these delights thy minde may moue,
Then liue with mee, and be my loue.

FINIS

Chr. Marlow.

XIX. CONCLUSION

"With Marlowe there came to the English stage a steady stream of light that proclaimed the new order of things. One after another, he showered his benefits upon the stage. He created the noblest vehicle of dramatic expression of which any language is capable; he created in "Edward II" a new type of play; he annihilated the classical drama, he annihilated the vernacular drama; and in place of them, he substituted something infinitely richer than men had ever dreamed of, something that appealed to all classes, that teemed with life and passion, that gathered into itself all the intellectual power and vigor of the people, something, in a word, that could be - as the classical drama could not, as the vernacular drama could not - the supreme and final expression of all that men had thought, and did, and suffered. He had, in fact, solved the problem with which we started. He had shown how the stage could be, and should be, in the very widest sense, a national institution."[1]

1. Verity, A.W.: Marlowe's Influence on Shakespeare's Early Style, page 83-84.

BIBLIOGRAPHY

C. Marlowe: Works, ed. by Rev. A.Dyce, London, 1859

ed. by A.H.Bullen, London, 1885, 3 vols.

ed. by C.F.Tucker Brooke, Oxford, 1929.

C. Marlowe: Plays, ed. by Havelock Ellis, London, Benn Ltd, 192?

Poems of Robert Greene, Christopher Marlowe and Ben Jonson, ed. by Robert Bell, London, Bell, 1876.

Simpson, Percy: The 1604 text of Marlowe's "Doctor Faustus", in "Essays and Studies" by members of the English Association, vol.7, page 144-153. Oxford, 1921.

Seaton, Ethel: Marlowe's Map, in "Essays and Studues", by members of the English Assoc., vol. 10, pp. 13-35. Oxford, 1924.

Ellis-Fermor, U.M.:"Tamburlaine, the Great", London, 1930.

Tucker-Brooke, C.F: Life of Christopher Marlowe, London, 1929.

Marks, J.P: Christopher Marlowe (play). Boston, Houghton, 1901.

Henslowe's Diary, ed. by W.W. Greg, London, Bullen, 1907.

Boas, F.S: Marlowe and his Circle, London, Oxford Univ. Press, 1931.

Tucker-Brooke, C.F: The Marlowe Canon, in "Modern Language Assoc. of Amer. Publ., vol. 37, page 367-417, 1922.

Boas, F.S: University Drama in the Tudor Age, London, 1914.

Baker, G.P: Dramatic Technique in Marlowe, in "Essays and Studies", by members of the English Assoc., vol.4, pg. 172-82,Oxford, 1913.

Hotson, J.L: Marlowe among the Churchwardens; in "Atlantic Monthly", July, 1926, page 37-44.

Smith, Moore: Marlowe at Cambridge, in "Modern Language Review", 1910.

Harvard Classics, ed. by C.W. Eliot, vol.19, page 197-243.

Tannenbaum, Dr.: The Assassination of C. Marlowe, London, 1928.

Lowell, J.R: The Old English Dramatists, Boston, Houghton, 1892.

Chambers, E.K. The Elizabethan Stage, Oxford, 1923.

Daighton, K: The Old Dramatists: Conjectural Readings, 1896.

Gray, Austin K: Some Observations on C. Marlowe as a Government Agent, in "Modern Language Assoc", Sept. 1928.

Ingram, J.H: Marlowe and his Poetry, London, Richards, 1906.

Seaton, Ethel: Marlowe, Robert Poley and the Tippings, in "Review of English Studies", July, 1929.

Boas, F.S: Shakespeare and his Predecessors, London, 1930.

Verity, A.W: Marlowe's Influence on Shakespeare's Early Style, London, 1886.

Madden, D.L: Shakespeare and His Fellows, New York, Dutton, 1916.

Hotson, J.L: The Death of Christopher Marlowe, London, 1925.

Chambers, E.K: Dramatic records from the Lansdowne Manuscripts, in Malone Society, Collections, vol.1, part 2, page 143-215, Oxford, 1908.

Chambers, E.K: Dramatic records from the Privy Council Register, Oxford, 1911.

Forsythe, R.S: The Passionate Shepherd" and English Poetry," in "Modern Language Assoc. of Amer. Publ., vol.40, pg. 692-742, Menasha, 1925.

Heywood, Thomas: Hierarchie of the Blessed Angels, London, Islop, 1635.

Heywood, Thomas: An Apology for Actors, London, Okes, 1612.

Lightning Source UK Ltd.
Milton Keynes UK
UKHW012000021218
333216UK00013B/1780/P

9 780265 589656